Praise for *Light of Setting Suns*

Few books have inspired and challenged me as profoundly as *Light of Setting Suns*. Only an author who knows aging from decades of academic research and ninety years of purposeful living could offer such authentic glimmers of light and hope for people of all ages. This book will be my companion as I live toward my own setting suns, and I commend it to others who want to live with meaning and purpose at every age.

—Bishop (Retired) Kenneth L. Carder
Ruth W. and A. Morris Williams Distinguished
Professor Emeritus of The Practice of Christian Ministry, Duke
Divinity School

When I think of aging with resiliency and faith, I think of my friend Dr. Richard Morgan. His heart and mind, like fields described in a hymn by Isaac Watts, "stand dressed in living green," speaking grace and wisdom afresh in his latest work. Readers surely will find their own spirits stirred as he leads us in these meditations through verdant fields of soul-se

—Daniel C. Potts, MD, FAAN
ist, Tuscaloosa VA Medical Center
Tuscaloosa, Alabama

Most of us will not live to scan the horizons and landscapes presented in a tenth decade of life. Through grace, Richard Morgan has arrived at that unfamiliar place; and in thoughtful, compassionate, tough-minded meditations, he tells us the amazing things he sees: That through it all, God is also there. We gratefully receive his gift: It is a brave triumph.

—Thomas Ronald Vaughan, M.Div., M.A., D.Min.
Author, retired pastor, and healthcare administrator

Having begun now his tenth decade, Richard Morgan's lively writing grips us with his knowledge of scripture, theology, and the wisdom of the ancients in regard to aging—and especially by his humor, often self-deprecating. Morgan's book will greatly assist professional counselors, clergy, lay shepherds, grown children of older adults, and the aged themselves as well as their caregivers.

—Dr. Dwyn M. Mounger
Author, retired clergy

In his latest book, Richard Morgan wrestles brilliantly and honestly with the challenges and possibilities of life at ninety. He shares hard-earned wisdom and a vision of a later life of purpose. A must read for anyone striving to live with hope and meaning at any age.

—Virginia Biggar
Executive Director | Communities Program Director
A-LIST | www.usagainstalzheimers.org

As the son of a mother in her nineties and as pastor of a large congregation with many older adults and caregivers, I find this book a helpful companion for the aging journey. There is a Good Shepherd who shows up in these pages. While the valleys full of fears are named, ultimately, it is faith that is claimed. Frailty is not the focus of this book. Richard's words capture the wonder at how old bones can surprise and rise with power and hope.

—Donovan Drake, M.Div., D.Min.
Pastor and head of staff,
Westminster Presbyterian Church, Nashville, TN

LIGHT *of* SETTING SUNS

REFLECTING ON REALITIES AND MYSTERIES
AT NINETY YEARS OF LIFE

RICHARD L. MORGAN

UPPER
ROOM BOOKS®
NASHVILLE

Library of Congress Cataloging-in-Publication Data

Names: Morgan, Richard Lyon, 1929- author.
Title: Light of setting suns : reflecting on realities and mysteries at
   ninety years of life / Richard L. Morgan.
Description: Nashville, TN : Upper Room Books, 2021. | Includes
   bibliographical references and index. |
Identifiers: LCCN 2020034552 (print) | LCCN 2020034553 (ebook) | ISBN
   9780835819541 (paperback) | ISBN 9780835819558 (mobi) | ISBN
   9780835819565 (epub)
Subjects: LCSH: Older people--Religious life. | Older people--Prayers and
   devotions. | Aging--Religious aspects--Christianity.
Classification: LCC BV4580 .M575 2021 (print) | LCC BV4580 (ebook) | DDC
   204/.40846--dc23
LC record available at https://lccn.loc.gov/2020034552
LC ebook record available at https://lccn.loc.gov/2020034553

Print ISBN: 978-0-8358-1954-1
Mobi ISBN: 978-0-8358-1955-8
Epub ISBN: 978-0-8358-1956-5

Printed in the United States of America

*In loving memory of my wife, Alice Ann Morgan;
and to my daughter, Anna Sever, whose support and
encouragement helped make this book a reality.*

*And to all ninety-years-old and older persons, who, like me,
are striving to live up to death.*

CONTENTS

FOREWORD

There is an old joke about a professor introduced to an audience with praise for "his last book," whereupon the professor leaps up to say, "*Latest*, not *last!*" I have no idea whether the book you hold in your hands ultimately will be the "latest" or the "last" book from Richard Morgan. But I do have certainty that it is a message from "a foreign country," a country most of us have not visited. In that respect, this book is uniquely valuable—indeed, indispensable.

How do we approach the last chapter of life, the time of advanced old age? After having spent nearly fifty years working with elders myself, I now find myself, at age seventy-five, still puzzled about the answer. Where better to go for guidance than those further advanced along the road of life? That is exactly the sentiment expressed by Socrates in the opening words of Plato's *The Republic*: "There is nothing which for my part I like better . . . than conversing with aged men; for I regard them as travelers who have gone a journey which I too may have to go, and of whom I ought to enquire."[1] Socrates's advice was never more appropriate than today, and Richard Morgan's book is an answer for us all.

In today's society, most of what is thought of as old age is something to be avoided or at least postponed. The strategy of *postponement* has a name: "compression of morbidity."[2] It is a wish to postpone any deficits of age until a later time. This strategy is an attractive one. But with any experience of life, we also know that "successful aging" is not always within our power. We may reach the ranks of advanced elderhood and experience losses: death of friends and family, chronic illness, loss of roles and connections with the wider world.

It is possible to prepare for losses, and so a second "P," the strategy of *preparation*, has much to recommend it. We can purchase long-term care insurance, redesign a home for "aging-in-place," and stay connected with friends and family. Preparation is not denial but rather anticipation of decrements and losses. The best definition of "successful aging" is "decrement with compensation."

But compensation does not always work. Postponement and preparation are necessary but not sufficient. There is a third "P," which leads us to the message of Richard Morgan's book. The third "P" is *pondering*, and it is best described as a spiritual, existential, or philosophical approach to later life. Our culture, alas, has little appreciation for pondering. This lack of appreciation is nothing new. It was long ago described in the New Testament, where it is symbolized by the contrasting figures of Martha and Mary (see Luke 10:38-42). This classic text is the origin, in Christian tradition, of the contrast between the so-called "active" life and the "contemplative" life, as represented by Martha and Mary. The point here is not to exalt contemplation over action but to note that Martha, with her active nature, simply cannot understand the more contemplative Mary.

There is much to be said in favor of "active aging," "productive aging," and all the other strategies that can help us extend midlife into old age. Rationality and problem-solving have their value. Yet most of us know that, at some point, strategies of postponement and preparation will fail. Then comes the time of pondering, if we can learn to hear the voice of Mary.

There is a literature of first-person accounts of death and dying—for example, Paul Kalanithi's *When Breath Becomes Air*, part of a wider literature of physicians writing about their own illness. But where are the first-person accounts by scholars of aging writing about their own experience among the "oldest-old"? It is rare, indeed—such a message from this foreign country that few of us have visited. It is the voice of Mary, even if Martha cannot quite understand what she is pondering.

As I said before, Richard Morgan's book is indispensable. The book is its own answer to the question, "Why am I still here?"

—Harry R. (Rick) Moody,
Distinguished Visiting Professor,
Fielding Graduate University, Santa Barbara, CA,
Editor, *Human Values in Aging* newsletter

FOREWORD

My dear friend, colleague, and coauthor Richard Lyon Morgan has done it again: The author of a treasury of books and articles, Richard, at ninety, has produced the best work of his long lifetime.

From the depths of his soul's understanding, Richard speaks with full authority about the risks and benefits of being and living among the "oldest-old" and seeks meaning in all of the events of each long day. The theme of the book is expressed in 2 Corinthians 4:16, where the apostle Paul asserts that, "Though our bodies are dying, our spirits are being renewed every day" (NLT).

Throughout almost thirty years of friendship and collaboration, Richard and I have ruminated on the meaning of that biblical passage for our own lives and for the elders we serve. Some elders live relatively unscathed by later life; others live ravaged by it. Few of us know (or want to know) how our old age will "play out." It is a mystery to be lived. No matter how many helpful books (even those that are research-based) or articles we read about the "aging process" and "how to age successfully," almost all of them are based on younger writers' observations of people they'd like to emulate as they age. By reflecting on and sharing his experiences at ninety, Richard provides us with an unadorned "insider's" viewpoint on the struggles that can come in old age.

For example, during the early months of the COVID-19 pandemic, Richard and his wife, Alice Ann, who in recent years have both been dealing with ill health and increasing frailty, had to relocate to a facility offering more assistance in a town an hour away from their previous residence, leaving behind friends and caregivers and starting over again.

Throughout such loss-filled changes, Richard has never stopped trying to find or create meaning in each day's events, trying to discover ways to "renew his spirit"—as well as the spirits of whomever he encounters. What he has found and what he offers us—firsthand—is that there is *hope*. He does not offer optimism that external events will change for the better but spiritual hope that no matter what happens, meaning can be made and love is available—if we choose to live it.

—Jane Marie Thibault MA, MSSW, PhD
Clinical Professor Emerita,
Dept. of Family and Geriatric Medicine,
School of Medicine, University of Louisville, KY

ACKNOWLEDGMENTS

More people than I could possibly name and thank have enabled me to write this book.

I am thankful to Upper Room Books Editorial Director Joanna Bradley Kennedy, who first endorsed my book and was a constant source of encouragement in the early stages of writing.

Thanks also to my editor, Joseph Crowe, whose careful and consistent editing helped to smooth out the rough places. His invaluable help in the editing process helped birth this book.

I am indebted to colleagues Jane Thibault and Harry (Rick) Moody, who wrote powerful forewords that gave new life to the book.

Friends Lynda Everman and Don Wendorf stood by me with support and encouragement from the beginning of writing the book to its completion.

Special thanks to the following friends and writers who graciously added their contributions to these pages: Lynda Everman, John C. Morgan, Danny C. Potts, David Seymour, Jane Thibault, Ronald Vaughan, and Don Wendorf.

I also wish to thank all of those ninety-or-older persons mentioned in the book. They generously provided the stories that gave my book meaning.*

And my thanks to Bob, Dorothy, Frank, Grandmother, Howard, Margaret, Marion, and all those who remain unnamed.

All of the author's royalties from the sale of this book will go to the Benevolent Care Fund at Redstone Highlands, a leading aging services network partner in Pennsylvania within the communities the organization serves.

PREFACE

That is why we never give up. Though our bodies are dying, our spirits are being renewed every day.

—2 Corinthinians 4:16, NLT

Thirty years ago, when I was sixty years old, I faced the unknown experience of my own aging. I searched for books of a spiritual nature to navigate me through the waters of this new experience. Only Kathleen Fischer's book *Winter Grace: Spirituality and Aging* spoke to me. Out of my own need, I wrote a book, *No Wrinkles on the Soul: A Book of Readings for Older Adults,* and sent it to Upper Room Books.

I will always be grateful that they took the risk of publishing this work by such an unknown writer. The book began a great relationship with Upper Room Books, in which I have written nine more books over the past twenty-nine years. I am now ninety years old, soon to be ninety-one, and I find myself once again in an unknown world. None of my previous books on aging seemed to resonate with what I was now experiencing. I searched for literature on this "oldest old" stage of life and found only a few works that were meaningful.

Ethicist Frits de Lange wrote a helpful book in 2015, *Loving Later Life: An Ethics of Aging.* In his book, de Lange wrote about the challenges facing the oldest old. Lars Tornstam, a

Swedish gerontologist, wrote about a positive view of later life, which he called "gerotranscendence." His book, *Gerotranscendence: A Developmental Theory of Positive Aging* (2005), was based on two decades of intensive study of much older people. This book deeply influenced me, as will be evident in what I have written.

However, both of these studies were written by "outsiders" who were researchers and scholars of these last years of life. None represented a book by an "insider" now ninety years old. At first, I thought it inconceivable, if not impossible, to write such a book. The years had taken their toll on my body, causing physical disabilities for which there is no cure. But my mind and spirit were still young! I was a witness to Paul's words, "That is why we never give up. Though our bodies are dying, our spirits are being renewed every day" (2 Cor. 4:16, NLT). I felt the presence of the Spirit, sometimes in the evening hours, urging me to attempt such a book.

So, I finally took up my pen and began to write how it feels to be ninety. The writing began on scraps of white paper, often while riding in my senior-living community's van to go grocery shopping or during endless hours of waiting in a doctor's office. At other times, I scribbled notes on napkins in the dining room of the community. There were moments when I would wake from sleep, the book on my subconscious mind, and jot down thoughts on a writing pad near my bed.

Soon, the writing project took shape, and ideas were transferred to my computer. I decided the book would have the same basic format as *No Wrinkles on the Soul*. It would consist of scripture readings, reflections by others, and my own meditations and prayers. My friends Don Wendorf and Lynda Everman came to my assistance when computer glitches caused problems, and they helped me prepare the manuscript.

I thought that this could be a valuable resource for the growing number of people on the cusp of being very old. They would learn what it feels like to be among the oldest old. It would offer insights to the great number of boomers, some of whom are not retired and some who soon will be. Adult children caring for aging parents might learn how to forge new relationships in these much later years of life.

The words of the mystic Meister Eckhart (c. 1260– c. 1328 CE) became a great inspiration for me in the process of writing this book:

> Above all else, then: Be prepared at all times
> for the gifts of God
> and be ready for new ones.
> For God is a thousand times more ready to give
> than we are to receive.[1]

Being Ninety

You never thought it would really happen, but all of a sudden you realize you actually are old and aging. You look in the mirror and see some old guy or your dad. First, you explain away why your balance is a bit off or why doors are heavier than they used to be or how the floor is a lot lower than before. You finally accept that you're now one of those "senior people." But just like at every other age, you still feel like you're "you" on the inside. You get issued only one *self*. Someone better take care of it and make the most of it, and it's probably going to have to be *you*.

—Don Wendorf

REACHING NINETY

The days of our life are seventy years,
    or perhaps eighty, if we are strong. . . .
So teach us to count our days
    that we may gain a wise heart.
—Psalm 90:10, 12

Scripture

Read Psalm 90:1-12.

Reflection

I'm just somebody who was born ninety years ago and will die in a few years' time and then everybody will have forgotten me. This is reality. We're all here, but we are just local people, passengers in a journey. We get into the train, we get out of the train, the train goes on.

—Jean Vanier,
founder of L'Arche Communities,
upon celebrating his ninetieth birthday[1]

Meditation

I find it hard to believe that I am ninety years old. By no stretch of my imagination did I think I would live this long. I have outlived all my ancestors except my maternal grandmother, who died at age ninety-two. I am sure that Moses, who may have written the ninetieth psalm, would change the words of verse 10, if he were living today. He would write that the years of our lives were eighty years, and ninety years, if by reason of strength.

Golda Meir, former prime minister of Israel, is reported to have said, "Being seventy is not a sin. It's not a joy, either." Being ninety has compounded for me earlier health issues caused by aging. Due to peripheral neuropathy, I am bound to a walker, and I leave the community in which I live only to do grocery shopping or go to doctors' appointments. My former wonderful days of travel have ended. Due to later-life digestive issues, I am on a restricted diet, which limits my joy in eating. My volunteer work with caregivers and people with dementia has lessened. I sometimes wonder why I am still here.

I admit, there are times when I succumb to the mournful cries of many people my age and wonder why the Lord has left me here so long. At times, I and they reflect the words of the patriarch Job, "They long for death, and it won't come. They search for death more eagerly than for hidden treasure" (3:21, NLT).

One of the few books written for later life is by Frits de Lange, *Loving Later Life: An Ethics of Aging*. I have read this book many times and find it greatly helpful for anyone living so long. De Lange defines loving later life as "accepting the call into the no-man's land of old age and surrendering oneself heartily to the opportunity of deepening the experience of being alive—up to death."[2] Unlike de Lange, I write not as a researcher or a scholar of later life but as one who is experiencing being ninety. Despite some diminishment, I am still "vital and green" (Ps. 92:14, NLT). As a pioneer of those being numbered among "the oldest old," what I write will surely deepen my experience of being alive, as well as, I hope, help others in this growing age cohort.

Prayer

Companion God, you have been my constant friend all these years. I am sure you will not forsake me now, when so much has been taken from me. Amen.

2

NOT YET

Wisdom will multiply your days and add years
to your life.

—Proverbs 9:11, NLT

Scripture

Read Deuteronomy 34:1-12.

Reflection

In the past twenty years or so, scientists have found that the
maximum natural human life span is approximately 120
years; some researchers believe it is even longer than that.
For the first time in the history of humankind, we (or our
children and grandchildren) may have the opportunity to
live that long. In the past century, we have added years to our
lives at an unprecedented rate.

—Jane Marie Thibault and Richard L. Morgan[3]

Meditation

A tourist could not find a friend's home in a rural area. He spied an old farmer mending a fence. He asked the farmer for directions to his friend's home. The farmer, who seemed old, recognized that home and told the tourist how to find it. The tourist wanted to be sure that the farmer's directions were accurate, so he asked him, "Have you lived here all your life?" The farmer replied, "Not yet!"

We are living much longer in America. The very old, those over eighty-six, are one of the fastest-growing age groups. This group numbered 4 million in the United States in the year 2000, projected to grow to nearly 9 million by 2050. This aged segment of the population, we are told, will grow from 12 percent to 21 percent, compared with 1900, when those sixty-five and older made up only 4 percent of the total US population.[4]

What some call the "gray tsunami" has swept upon us. This phrase suggests a terrifying vision of a giant wave of old people on the horizon. Medical science has extended our life span beyond our fondest dreams. At times, I pinch myself to convince myself I am really ninety years old. At my final sermon in an African American church in North Carolina, the congregation dedicated a song to me, "Still Here"; and twenty years later, I am *still* here!

However, the marvels of medical technology may well have extended our years, but they cannot tell us how to live these years or what it means to live so long. It is only through the life of the Spirit that we discover why we have lived so long. I have learned that living this long means accepting whatever that oldest age brings and deepening these years with enrichment and joy. In this way, I can be a witness to others who will, like me, live long lives.

The words of Alfred, Lord Tennyson have lived with me for many years, but they mean even more now that I am ninety:

> Old age hath yet his honour and his toil;
> Death closes all: but something ere the end,
> Some work of noble note, may yet be done.[5]

That is my prayer every day.

Prayer

Lord of all ages, I feel blessed that you have given me these bonus years. Help me to live each day as if it were my last, redeeming whatever time remains. Amen.

Ninth Stage of Life

He asked you to preserve his life,
and you granted his request.
The days of his life stretch on forever.
—Psalm 21:4, NLT

Scripture

Read Psalm 21.

Reflection

Wisdom is not what comes from reading books. When it comes to understanding life, experiential learning is the only worthwhile kind, everything else is hearsay.
—Joan Erikson[6]

Meditation

Erik and Joan Erikson believed that there was another stage of life beyond the eight stages in Erik Erikson's theory of development. They became aware that many people were living into their eighties and nineties, and their eighth stage of life, as it had been classified, did not relate to the issues and challenges people faced when they were much older.

The Eriksons defined a ninth stage of life, characterized by diminishments and losses not experienced in earlier stages. Joan Erikson, who died at ninety-five, believed that in the ninth stage of life, people were more likely to be concerned with what body part might not be working that day or what friend might be gone tomorrow. Furthermore, people in this stage could experience loss of identity when their autonomy was taken away by their children.

Despite these challenges, Joan Erikson believed that older people can overcome them and gain wisdom. This wisdom is related to realizing the meaning of one's life story. She used the metaphor of a woven fabric to describe the life story.[7] She believed that the threads attached to a loom before the weaving represented a person's core. The weft or crosswise threads that are woven back and forth to complete the fabric represented life's experiences.

Wisdom, at this ninth stage, begins where experience ends; wisdom is experience well digested. Joan Erikson believed that much-older persons can transcend the difficulties and challenges they will inevitably confront and attain wisdom.

Prayer

Most wise God, grant me the strength and courage to overcome all the difficulties being very old brings and grant me the wisdom garnered by experiencing them. Amen.

WISDOM PEOPLE

[The older men] answered [Rehoboam], "If you will be a servant to this people today and serve them, and speak good words to them when you answer them, then they will be your servants forever." But [Rehoboam] disregarded the advice that the older men gave him.

—1 Kings 12:7-8

Scripture

Read 1 Kings 12:1-19.

Reflection

When we looked at the life cycle in our 40s, we looked to old people for wisdom. At 80, though, we look at other 80-year-olds to see who got wise and who not. Lots of old people don't get wise, but you don't get wise unless you age.

—Joan Erikson[8]

Meditation

The Yoruba tribe of Nigeria call their old people "wisdom people." According to oral tradition, they believe that when a knowledgeable old person dies, a whole library's worth of information disappears. In other past societies, the old people were called "elders" because it was recognized that having lived so long, they had harvested wisdom.

The Bible records at least two moments in holy history when the wisdom of older people played a prominent role. At a crucial moment in Israel's history, King Rehoboam, son of Solomon, did not listen to the wisdom of older men. These men tried to persuade the king to take a softer approach to the people, but he rejected their wisdom. Instead, he took the counsel of younger men, who demanded a hard approach, and that plunged the nation into a civil war. It is older people, who have lived through good and bad decisions of the past, who have gained wisdom to consider alternatives.

In another moment of holy history, the wisdom of the aged Gamaliel saved the apostles' lives. While other members of the Sanhedrin wanted to execute the apostles, Gamaliel wisely advised caution. For if the disciples of Jesus represented a false movement, Gamaliel argued, it would soon vanish; but if their work was indeed of God, no one could stop it. This time, the authorities did listen to the wisdom of an older person (see Acts 5:12-42).

We cannot expect wisdom from the young, for they have simply not lived long enough or been through enough to have been able to acquire wisdom. One learns by living; and the longer one lives, the more the likelihood of his or her having understanding and insight deepens. Wisdom is the art of living in rhythm with your soul, your life, and God. Even today, our world would be well advised to listen to and accept the wisdom of older people.

Prayer

Wise God, grant to us in our later years the wisdom that James, the brother of Jesus, described as "pure, then peaceable, gentle, willing to yield, full of mercy and good fruits, without a trace of partiality or hypocrisy" (James 3:17). Amen.

WISDOM KEEPERS

You shall rise before the aged, and defer to
the old; and you shall fear your God: I am the
LORD.

—Leviticus 19:32

Scripture

Read Isaiah 51:1-3.

Reflection

May the warm winds of heaven blow softly upon your house.
May the Great Spirit bless all who enter there.
May your moccasins make happy tracks in many snows,
and may the rainbow always touch your shoulder.

—Cherokee Prayer Blessing

Meditation

Several years ago, I went to the Cherokee Reservation in Western North Carolina to do research on Native American history. I hadn't yet met anyone who could tell me about the kind of history I was most interested in, so one of the people I met advised me to visit a certain old woman who lived by herself. I drove down an old country road and spotted an elderly, white-haired Native American woman, sitting on the porch and smoking a corncob pipe.

Cautiously, I approached her and asked if we could talk. "No one visits me anymore," she said. "So, I am glad for company." Then she grinned from her toothless mouth and said, "You can call me Grandmother. That's the name they gave me. They say I'm over ninety years old, but I have lost count of the years." I asked her about her family and how long she had lived there. "Family is gone, I am the only one left. My parents hid in these backwoods to escape the forced migration of the tribe to Oklahoma. I have lived here ever since."

She paused, still puffing on her pipe, as her mind seemed far away. Then, she went on. "It all seems a blur now," she said. "But some memories still linger. I remember how the wisdom keepers would sit in a circle before a blazing fire and share their wisdom. I was young then, but their words are still with me." She sighed and added, "No one asks me any-more about those days. Soon, even I will forget." After a few more words, she spoke no more. I thanked her and drove away, leaving her still sitting on the porch.

As I left her, I could not escape a feeling of sadness that this remarkable old woman lived in such isolation. Soon, her stories of the past would be lost when she died. She was truly a "wisdom keeper," but soon, that history would die with her.

Prayer

Ancient of Days, I will always be grateful for people like Grandmother, whose wisdom is so valuable. Help us find ways to keep that wisdom alive. Amen.

6

THE BEST IS LAST

"Everyone serves the good wine first, and then the inferior wine . . . [b]ut you have kept the good wine until now."

—John 2:10

Scripture

Read John 2:1-12.

Reflection

As for old age, embrace and love it. It abounds with pleasure if you know how to use it. The gradually declining years are among the sweetest in a [person's] life, and I maintain that, even when they have reached the extreme limit, they have their pleasure still. . . .

Life is most delightful on the downward slope.

—Seneca the Younger (c. 4 BCE–65 CE)[9]

Meditation

In the 1980s, the Swedish gerontologist Lars Tornstam developed a theory of aging called *gerotranscendence*. In a study that took more than twenty years, Tornstam interviewed many older people in Sweden, ages sixty-five through 104. He found that many of these older people had not succumbed to a negative view of aging; instead, they had transcended the view that being old is all doom and gloom and had achieved a positive view of being old.

Tornstam found that many of the older people he interviewed had a decreased interest in material things and preferred solitude. They were less self-occupied, while also being more selective about their social activities, and they felt they needed only a few friends. These older people also had an increased feeling of universal togetherness, where past memories become present reality. Also, those who were gerotranscendent believed in a mystery about the universe, and even death had a different meaning for them.

Could it be that the last years may well be our best years? It was surely a fact that the best wine at the wedding feast in Cana was the last wine. The master of ceremonies was astounded that the water Jesus changed into wine was better than the expensive wine he had served first. In a similar way, the last years may be our best! The poet Robert Browning thought so:

> Grow old along with me!
> The best is yet to be,
> The last of life, for which the first was made.[10]

Prayer

God of life, I pray that we may experience the truth that our last years will be our best. Amen.

7

A STRIKING CONTRAST

"They long for death, and it won't come.
  They search for death more eagerly than for
    hidden treasure. . . .
But I don't have the strength to endure.
  I have nothing to live for."
—Job 3:21; 6:11, NLT

The glory of the young is their strength;
  the gray hair of experience is the splendor of
    the old.
—Proverbs 20:29, NLT

Scripture

Read Job 3; Proverbs 20.

Reflection

Life and circumstances may not go your way. In fact, if you live long enough, you will undoubtedly experience this more than once in your life. But regardless of the situation and your age, you always have a choice. You can choose to live life fully and generously, to think of others, and to give back. Or you can become mired in your own grief, regrets, and disappointments. At times, it will take courage, determination, and the willingness to accept help, but the choice is yours. Choose to live with hope.

—Lynda Everman

Meditation

Observe the contrast between two women, both ninety-nine years old and living in a retirement community. One sits in a lonely room in Personal Care. She is crabby and demanding, and she makes her caregivers' lives miserable. Reluctantly, she goes to activities, usually with a scowl on her face. Her only daughter tries to visit her, but their time together becomes so unpleasant, the daughter visits less often now. She hates her life, only wants to be left alone, and doesn't want to go on living. For her, old age means decline and bitterness. She constantly complains about having lived so long, and she dreads every day, as she waits for a death that never seems to come.

In the same community, another woman, also ninety-nine years old, is still in Independent Living and has accepted care from aides with a cheerful smile. They all love her and respect her. Once a week, she supervises a walking club's visit to a park. As others walk, she is content to sit in a pavilion and watch the walkers. She enjoys being outside and revels in the beauty of nature. She still reads novels and enjoys people. Originally from New England, she loves to quote a line from Robert Frost's poem "Stopping by Woods on a Snowy Evening": "But I have promises to keep, and miles to go before I sleep." Her snow-white hair exemplifies what the writer of Proverbs meant by saying, "The gray hair of experience is the splendor of the old."

Two women, both ninety-nine years old, both with physical restrictions, but what a difference in their perspectives! One chooses a complaining, self-defeating attitude; one chooses a positive, accepting attitude. It might be circumstantially harder for the first to have a better attitude, but we always have some choice here, and the choice makes a huge difference.

Prayer

Father of mercies, as the losses and illnesses of being very old enter my life, help me meet these demands with smiles, not scowls. Amen.

HAPPINESS IS
A CHOICE YOU MAKE

"I call heaven and earth to witness against you today that I have set before you life and death, blessings and curses. Choose life."

—Deuteronomy 30:19

Scripture

Read Deuteronomy 30:11-20.

Reflection

One of the few advantages of age is that you can report on it with a certain authority; you are a native now, and know what goes on here. . . . Our experience is one unknown to most of humanity, over time. We are the pioneers.

—Penelope Lively[11]

Meditation

Recently, author John Leland interviewed and lived among six New Yorkers, most of whom were ninety years old or older then or are by now. As he says of them, "They belonged to one of the fastest-growing age groups in America, now so populous that they had their own name: the oldest old."[12] Leland had expected hearing stories of negativity and of their declining health and loneliness, if not despair. All had experienced major losses in their very old age, but they had learned to live with them and to enjoy the last years of life.

Leland writes, "One of the great mysteries of old age is why some people . . . continue to grow and thrive long after their peers wind down."[13] One reason why some of the very old thrive is that they have found a purpose in life. For them, life is still worth living, not a seemingly endless wait for death. These elders were living more fulfilling years, even though age had taken its toll.

What this means for me is that in these very later years, happiness is a choice we who are the oldest old must make. I live in a retirement community where the average age is ninety-one, with some residents ninety-nine years old and one man who is 102. Some, even here, choose to whine and decline. But others focus on making the most of life, despite its limitations. Their optimistic and positive life is a witness to us all.

Prayer

Lord, you give us the same choice you gave the children of Israel—to choose life or death. Give us grace to accept life and still find happiness in these extended years. Amen.

Becoming Oneself
at Ninety

I t is a fascinating pursuit in itself, and our efforts will not have been wasted if they help us to possess our own identities as an artist possesses his work. At least we can say to the world of the future, or to ourselves if nobody else will listen, "I really *was*"—or even, with greater self-confidence, "I was and am *this*."

—Malcolm Cowley[1]

Decreased
Self-Centeredness

If anyone is in Christ, there is a new creation:
everything old has passed away; see, everything
has become new!

—2 Corinthians 5:17

Scripture

Read 2 Corinthians 5:16-21.

Reflection

Christ—Our New Identity

The ultimate goal of our seeking and growing in God's love
in this lifetime is to be able to say, as St. Paul said, "It is no
longer I who live, but it is Christ who lives in me" (Gal. 2:20).
Our True Self is not a mere psychological achievement—it
is the realization that we are called to a new identity and

have been given a new reason for being (no matter what our age or external circumstances). Mystical theologians call this "transformation in Christ." Once we have discarded our false self and embraced our True Self, we discover a challenging new life awaits us—and it's here on Earth.

We are called to become another Christ gift to the world.

—Jane Marie Thibault

Meditation

There was a time in my life when I was so self-centered that I was fearful of what others thought of me and always seeking the approval of other people. My poor self-concept was due to an authoritarian father and a tradition that scripted me from birth. I felt I had to be what my family wanted me to be, not what I wanted to be. I went to seminary, burdened with this "false self." In the parish ministry, I felt the need for approval by authority figures, and I found myself either as a victim of power struggles or of my own foolish rebellion.

At last, I found the courage to leave the parish ministry. I was not defrocked but "unsuited"! I chose my new way as a college teacher and writer. I found myself. The truth set me free (see John 8:32)! I realized what Thomas Merton meant by distinguishing between the "false self" (what others want you to be) and the "true self" (who I choose to be). The apostle Paul wrote, "By the grace of God I am what I am" (1 Cor. 15:10).

Now, in my very old years, I love my old self. This is authentic self-love, not selfishness. I am no longer concerned or worried about what other people think about me, nor do I seek their approval. My conviction is, "Take me or leave me; that's the way it is!" I am reminded of Paul's counsel to the church at Philippi: "Do nothing from selfish ambition or conceit, but in humility regard others as better than yourselves. Let each of you look not to your own interests but to the interests of others" (Phil. 2:3-4).

This self-acceptance has liberated me to relate with freedom and joy to all people, especially those with dementia. They won't even know my name, but being with them as a non-anxious presence confirms my true self.

Prayer

Lord of love, you taught us to love others as we love ourselves. I am grateful for the freedom to be who I am and to love others too. Amen.

10

It's OK to Be Useless

Happy are those . . .
. . . .
[whose] delight is in the law of the Lord,
and on his law they meditate day and night.
They are like trees
planted by streams of water,
which yield their fruit in its season,
and their leaves do not wither.
In all that they do, they prosper.

—Psalm 1:1-3

Scripture

Read Psalm 1.

Reflection

A carpenter said to his apprentice, "Do you know why this tree is so big and so old?" The apprentice said, "No, why?"

The carpenter answered, "Because if it were useful, it would have been cut and sawed up and used for beds and tables.

"But because it is useless, it has been allowed to grow. That is why it is now so great, that you can rest in its shadow."

—Taoist parable

Meditation

I went to see my old friend Howard. I had moved to another town and had not seen him for some time. I sat with Howard in rocking chairs on the porch, as we talked about old times. Howard had been an active person, managed a rest home, and did volunteer work. Now, however, being very old and with many physical problems, he had stopped driving. He had to rely on neighbors to do his grocery shopping for him and his wife and to take them both to their doctors.

I listened to Howard's lament, as he said, "I used to be an active person, busy as a bee, and always helping other people. Now I just sit on the porch and stare into space. I feel so useless. Managing a garden was always such a joy for me in these retirement years, but now I am so feeble, my friends plant my garden."

As we sat in silence, I remembered a Taoist parable about an old tree. It seemed to fit the moment, so I shared the parable of what seemed like a useless, old tree but still had value. I felt it might speak to Howard.

Howard listened intently and got the message. He smiled and said, "Well, I've had a good life and many wonderful friends. Maybe the time has come to sit back and do nothing, and hopefully, others like you will come and sit with me and find some rest." Howard seemed more resigned to being idle and accepting of his inactive life. It was the last time I ever saw my friend.

Prayer

Understanding God, help me to know I don't have to be productive any longer but that being "useless" can grant me much-needed rest and be a blessing in disguise. Amen.

11

BE YOUR OWN GOOD SAMARITAN

"You shall love the Lord your God with all your heart, and with all your soul, and with all your strength, and with all your mind; and your neighbor as yourself."

—Luke 10:27

Scripture

Read Luke 10:25-37.

Reflection

Today on my journey I met a man
named Myself,
injured and alone, lying by the roadside.
Some others had passed by.
Yet I stopped, knelt, and tended
the man I'd left to die one day before.

—Daniel C. Potts

Meditation

I was born in the Good Samaritan Hospital in Lexington, Kentucky, ninety years ago. Jesus' parable of the good Samaritan has followed me all my life. I have been a good Samaritan to many people in my life. On one occasion, I helped a distraught college student who was pregnant out of wedlock. She came to me when others passed her by, and I stood by her and performed her wedding. I reached out to a Vietnam veteran who was still traumatized by that war, and I spent many hours counseling him. I came to the side of many Black students, often alienated by a white society. Recently, I was there for people with dementia and their caregivers, as they struggled with this disease for which there is still no cure.

There have been moments in my long journey when others became good Samaritans for me, when life had robbed me of happiness and left me alone and wounded on the road of life. I have been immeasurably blessed by their kindness and support. I know my life would have been desolate without them. Now, as I face disabilities of old age, personal-care aides have helped me manage my frail body. My wife has been my good Samaritan, caring for me and propping me up on every leaning side, so I avoid a fall that could have dire consequences.

Now, I find myself among the very old. I believe the parable of the good Samaritan speaks to me in a new and different way. The priest and the Levite, who passed by the wounded man in the story, represent the part of me that attempts to pass by my emotional and spiritual needs. All my life, I have been so devoted to caring for others that I have often neglected my own needs. Loving my old soul means having compassion for my frail and feeble state. It's time to be good to myself, accepting my frailty, forgiving myself for wrongs I have done to others and the foolish choices I made in my life.

Some time ago, my oldest son, Rick, now sixty-five years old, gave me a bookmark on Father's Day that had this message:

TAKE TIME TO BE AS GOOD TO YOURSELF
AS YOU ARE TO OTHERS.

That time is now!

Prayer

Thank you, Jesus, that you are the true good Samaritan. May I treat myself as you would treat me. Amen.

12

LESS CONCERNED WITH POSSESSIONS

[Jesus] said to them, "Take heed and beware of covetousness; for one's life does not consist in the abundance of the things he possesses."

—Luke 12:15, NKJV

Scripture

Read Luke 12:13-21.

Reflection

In the last century an American tourist visited the renowned Polish Rabbi Hofetz Chaim. The tourist was amazed to find the Rabbi's home only a simple room, filled with books, a table, and a bench. "Rabbi," he asked, "Where is your furniture?"

"Where is yours?" asked the Rabbi.

"Mine?" asked the puzzled American. "But I'm only a visitor here. I'm only passing through."

"So am I," replied the Rabbi.
—James A. Thorson and Thomas C. Cook, Jr.[2]

Meditation

I often look at the painting of the rich young ruler that hangs on the wall near my bed. As I look at the ruler's hands, I am not sure whether he is holding on to his wealth or letting it go. Most seem to believe he could not relinquish his wealth, and so he went away sorrowful. The ruler had so much wealth that he could not leave it behind and follow Jesus to a new life. It is all too easy to identify ourselves with material things.

The rich farmer in Jesus's parable in Luke 12 was possessed by his possessions. Apparently, he had acquired his wealth honestly and even planned to build bigger barns before retiring in style. But then, death knocked at his door, and he realized there are no pockets in shrouds or U-Haul trailers on hearses. As the patriarch Job observed, "Naked I came from my mother's womb, and naked shall I return there" (1:21).

What prevents us from a good life is clinging to or craving things. The Latin writer Cicero (106–43 BCE) wrote, "As for avariciousness in the old, what purpose it can serve I do not understand, for can anything be more absurd in the traveller than to increase his luggage as he nears his journey's end?"[3] I know all too well that the end of my life is near. Time is short, and every day is like the flipping pages of a calendar used in old movies to suggest the passing of time. I have never defined myself by what I own. I have never had many possessions, except my books; and even now, I am in the process of giving most of them away.

I take another look at the painting of the rich young ruler. I wonder if he had been a rich *old* ruler, aware that the end of his life was imminent, might he have given his money to the poor and followed Jesus? Or it may have been that the rich young ruler did heed Jesus' words, gave his wealth to the poor, and discovered a new identity as a disciple of Christ. I hope that the latter might be true. What really matters is that we "lay up for ourselves treasures in heaven" (Matt. 6:20, KJV, AP).

Prayer

God who speaks, let me hear your call not to be attached to what I have but to find my real treasure in being who I am and in the life in the Spirit. Amen.

Death Cleaning

We all come to the end of our lives as naked
and empty-handed as on the day we were born.
We can't take our riches with us.

—Ecclesiastes 5:15, NLT

Scripture

Read Matthew 6:19-21.

Reflection

Aging and approaching death involve a lot of loss and letting go—of abilities, relationships, choices, power, identity, influence. This usually includes possessions too: our
big house, the car that gave us independence, the musical
instruments we can no longer cart around or play, cherished
books, gifts from loved ones, and on and on. This can be
very hard, as these things have been marinating in memories for years and years. But at some point, we have to realize

that stuff is just stuff. What really matters is what we take with us: our self, our knowledge, our wisdom, the experience of all our years and relationships. Our kids will be glad we cleaned out the storeroom.

—Don Wendorf

Meditation

As I have reached the age of ninety, getting rid of my possessions has become crucial. It is mandated by the reality that death is not far away.

Swedish author Margareta Magnusson calls it "death cleaning." She claims it is a gift for your children and loved ones, so they don't have to deal with your possessions when you die. It is also a gift for oneself because clearing out the clutter is a cleansing experience.[4]

This process began for me in 2003, when my wife and I moved to a retirement community. We gave up our house and sold many of our possessions in a yard sale. Among the things that were discarded were Major League baseball caps I had collected over the years. I also gave many of my books to a seminary student or to the public library. And I had never had much furniture.

Since then, I have continued death cleaning. What had been a full bookcase of cherished books was downsized to only a few. I mainly kept books I had written or wanted to reread. Only a skeleton of my library remains. It was difficult to say goodbye to valued books that had helped me on my life's journey. I can only hope that someone will select them from the library's stacks and read them, but this may be wishful thinking in this age of books online.

Clothes and albums were next. Many of my clothes were donated to Goodwill Industries, and I seldom buy any new clothes. Photo albums of grandchildren were given to their parents. The Morgan-Lyon family history, which took years of research to write, was given to my two sons. I have kept my memoirs, because I want to read them again to rekindle old memories of my life story, especially as some of those memories I can no longer recall.

As time goes on, more of my stuff will go. Death cleaning is a cleansing experience, and it prepares the soul for the final journey at death.

Prayer

From all tyranny to things and being possessed by my possessions, continue to deliver me, O God, in these last years of my life. Grant me the awareness that all I take into the next world is who I am, not what I have. Amen.

14

TRANSCENDING
DIMINISHMENT

We can rejoice, too, when we run into problems and trials, for we know that they help us develop endurance. And endurance develops strength of character.

—Romans 5:3-4, NLT

Scripture

Read Romans 5:1-11.

Reflection

A spirituality of aging must help us find a way to turn losses into gains, to learn how the stripping process which often accompanies aging can be a gradual entrance into freedom and new life, how, in fact, aging can be winter grace. . . . Winter grace is courage grown larger in the face of diminishment.

—Kathleen Fischer[5]

Meditation

There is no doubt that people who live into their eighties and nineties will face diminishment. I am among those whose frailties cause me to belong to what Harry R. (Rick) Moody calls the "illderly."[6] I cannot agree with those who promote a "new old age," remaining youthful in old age. Rather, I agree with the term "real old age."[7] There has been no discovery of the Fountain of Youth. The words of Ecclesiastes 12 ring true every day in very old age: "The days of trouble" (v. 1) are an ever-increasing reality.

Although I have reasonably good health at my advanced age, I am still a victim of failing sight and hearing and loss of mobility. Neuropathy confines me to a walker, and I live every day in mortal dread of losing my balance and falling, with the inevitable results that would follow. As one ninety-year-old man said, "What doesn't hurt doesn't work!" I suffer from arthritis, which limits the time I can spend using the computer. But I have no complaints, since so far, I have avoided heart disease, Alzheimer's disease, and cancer.

My friend Frank died at the age of 102. He had lost his sight and hearing and was a resident in memory care, a form of long-term care for people with Alzheimer's, dementia, or other types of memory problems. I remember how, when he still was a resident in independent living, he sat in the dining room one night, and when no one noticed him, he shouted, "Give me something to eat!" Another night, as I walked the halls, I had noticed Frank having problems getting into his apartment. So, I helped him open the door, and he slumped into his favorite chair. He turned on the TV, which he could neither see nor hear, but he told me that he would still cheer for his team! Even after he had become a new resident in memory care, he had still made his needs known.

Like Frank, many of the oldest old transcend their diminishments with courage and a defiant faith. They exemplify what Kathleen Fischer calls "winter grace," which she defines as "courage grown larger in the face of diminishment."[8] People like Frank are a witness to me, and they show the way to transcending diminishments.

Prayer

Lord of love, grant me courage to accept my trials, learn to endure them with patience, and realize that such courage and faith create character. Amen.

FACING THE WORST FEAR

"When you are old, you will stretch out your hands, and others will dress you and take you where you don't want to go."

—John 21:18, NLT

Scripture

Read John 21:18-19.

Reflection

Prayer at Ninety

O God,
It seems like yesterday
that I was eighty,
and now, at ninety,
I haven't much time left.
I can't shut my eyes to the fact
that I am very old and much frailer.

I know that among my greatest fears
is being sent to a nursing home
and becoming totally dependent on others.
Give me grace for these last years
and acceptance of whatever they may bring.
—Richard L. Morgan

Meditation

As a much older person facing innumerable health issues, I go to doctors quite often. It seems as though I have a different doctor for every organ of my body. Sitting in the waiting room can be a stressful experience, always wondering what the latest tests will reveal. Some call these anxiety-provoking visits the "white coat syndrome." One doctor, who saw many older people, told his receptionist to give each person a number to indicate when each would be called. The receptionist demurred, saying, "There's no way I'm going to tell those old people their number is up!"

I have been blessed thus far not to be diagnosed with any life-threatening illnesses, although repeated ministrokes have made me nervous about suffering a major stroke, which happened to several family members of mine. My worst fear is having to go to a nursing home. Anyone who lives beyond the age of eighty-five has about a 50 percent chance of ending up in a nursing home[9] and/or developing dementia. Think of two older people you know: Statistically speaking, one of them will go to a nursing home.

The words Jesus spoke to Simon Peter on the shores of Lake Galilee were designed to show Peter how he would die. But being taken where we do not want to go can also mean being taken to a nursing home, where older people are often forsaken and warehoused. I know very few old people who want to go to a nursing home. In those places, one becomes totally dependent upon others for constant care. So many of these residents just want to die, and they wonder why God has left them here so long.

If I have to be sent to a nursing home, I will try my best to accept this major life change and to rely on my courage and God's help to make the best of it. But I pray I will end my life in my "cell," surrounded by the presence of my wife, my books, and my family photos.

Prayer

O, God,
Thy sea is so great and my
boat is so small.
—Breton fisherman's prayer[10]

Episodic Memory

This day shall be a day of remembrance for you.
—Exodus 12:14

Remember the days of old,
consider the years long past.
—Deuteronomy 32:7

Scripture

Read Psalm 77.

Reflection

The fear of forgetting and the need to remember both mark the later years of life. . . . Memory enables us to hold fast to our identity and shape it in new ways. The Hebrew verb "to remember" means bringing the past into the present.
—Kathleen Fischer

Meditation

In later life, the barrier between the past and present is removed, and memories of the past become real in the present moment. Working memory—short-term memory—starts to fail, and I find myself forgetting names and appointments. But episodic memory, which is memory from specific experiences in one's life, is remembered from a first-person perspective. Since these memories last for a long time, they can be considered long-term memories. I have relived many memories from my long life. Among them are the following.

It was Christmas Eve 1957. I had participated in a midnight worship service, and the Methodist minister, with whom I had formed a strong friendship, invited me to the parsonage for coffee. For two hours, I listened as he vented feelings about problems in his parish. It was 2:00 a.m. when I walked on deserted streets to my home. It began to snow, and the world was filled with mystic beauty. It reminded me of that first "Silent Night" and Bethlehem. I began to sing to myself, "O little town of Bethlehem, how still we see thee lie; above thy deep and dreamless sleep the silent stars go by." That moment, so many years ago, became a recent reality. It was looking back to a past that no longer exists but an altogether new kind of time where everything that ever was continues to be.

It was 1964, and I was a chaplain at Peace College, an all-girls college in Raleigh, North Carolina. One of the students came to my office, distraught and anxious. She was pregnant and had not told her parents. I understood her predicament and performed a marriage ceremony for her and the solider whom she loved. Much later, she wrote and told me that they had a happy marriage and were blessed with three children. I thank God I could be there for this couple and be their good Samaritan.

The children of Israel celebrated the Passover not just as an ancient ritual but as a reminder that every generation would be present in that moment of freedom from bondage. At ninety, with more time for meditation, I often find myself reliving episodes from my life, which gives me joy as they come alive in the moment.

Prayer

Thank you, God, for blessed memories of my long life. Time vanishes, and those memories come alive, and I relive them with joy and thanksgiving. Amen.

Relating to Others
at Ninety

At times our own light goes out and is rekindled by a spark from another person. Each of us has cause to think with deep gratitude of those who have lighted the flame within us.

—Albert Schweitzer[1]

Just a Few Good Friends

Some friends play at friendship
 but a true friend sticks closer than one's
  nearest kin.
                            —Proverbs 18:24

Scripture

Read Proverbs 17:17.

Reflection

Think where man's glory most begins and ends,
And say my glory was I had such friends.
                            —W. B. Yeats[2]

I count myself in nothing else so happy
As in a soul remembering my good friends.
                            —William Shakespeare[3]

Meditation

One characteristic of very old people is that they become more selective with whom they spend their time. They are not actively looking for new friends or networking for new contacts. They value having just a few good friends with whom they can share their lives. I have learned that good friends are more gift than achievement. Over a lifetime, they have been few in number, and that is drastically evident in much later life.

The Celts called soul friends *anam cara*. The term originated in early Celtic Christianity and meant "one who shared my soul." Soul mates were often cell mates, who lived and worked together. A soul mate was a person to whom the inner self can be revealed, hiding nothing. Saint Brigid, abbess of the monastery at Kildaire, said, "A person without a soul friend is like a body without a head."[4]

Other than my wife, adult children, and brothers, I have just a few soul friends. Jane Thibault is a soul friend. Not only have we coauthored two books but we share thoughts and ideas via email or telephone. Although miles apart, she is my spiritual director, with whom I can share my innermost feelings in complete confidence.

Audrey was a soul friend. She was an amazing person with spiritual depth and with whom I could share beliefs and ideas. Her untimely death makes it difficult to have friends in this community, where death is ever-present.

Don and Lynda are soul friends. We have shared our mutual concern for people with dementia and their caregivers.

The writer of Proverbs said it well: "There are friends who pretend to be friends, but there is a friend who sticks closer than a brother" (18:24, RSV). I have been blessed with soul friends, especially at ninety.

Prayer

I thank you, God, for being my greatest friend. Amen.

AVOID BUSYNESS
AND BUSYBODIES

"'Guard this man; if he is missing, your life shall be given for his life. . . .' While your servant was busy here and there, he was gone."

—1 Kings 20:39-40

Scripture

Read 1 Timothy 5:9-13.

Reflection

To allow oneself to be carried away by a multitude of conflicting concerns, to surrender to too many demands, to commit oneself to too many projects, to want to help everyone in everything is to succumb to violence.

—Thomas Merton[5]

The Senility Prayer

Grant me the senility
To forget the people
I never liked anyway,
The good fortune
To run into the ones I do,
And the eyesight
To tell the difference.

—Ben Witherington[6]

Meditation

At the age of ninety, near the end of my life journey, I am more selective about how I spend my time and with whom I spend it. I avoid wasting precious time with superficial social contacts and instead spend more time in solitude. I agree with what Blaise Pascal wrote: "All men's miseries derive from not being able to sit in a quiet room alone."[7]

Unlike some social scientists who scramble to develop new ways for old people to keep busy, I avoid being busy. I shun large gatherings and prefer the quietness of my apartment, where I can spend time in meditation, listening to music, and spiritual reading. Unlike the servant of King Ahab, who got so busy he lost the soldier he was guarding (see 1 Kings 20:35-43), I want to guard my time in these final years.

The apostle Paul wrote to his young friend words of counsel for young men to avoid being "gossips and busybodies" (1 Tim. 5:13). Earlier, in his letter to the Thessalonians, Paul had written, "For we hear that some of you are living in idleness, mere busybodies, not doing any work" (2 Thess. 3:11).

I live in a retirement community, where there are a few people who are busybodies, majoring in minding other people's business. At times, they tear other people down to build themselves up. They seem to revel in talk about other people. I try to be polite to everyone here, but I avoid busybodies. At ninety years old, I am more concerned about surviving every day.

Prayer

Help me, gracious God, to redeem the time and to refrain from meaningless activities and thoughtless people. Amen.

19

More Blessed to Receive

Then [Jesus] poured water into a basin and began to wash the disciples' feet and to wipe them with the towel that was tied around him. He came to Simon Peter, who said to him, "Lord, are you going to wash my feet?" Jesus answered, "You do not know now what I am doing, but later you will understand." Peter said to him, "You will never wash my feet." Jesus answered, "Unless I wash you, you have no share with me."

—John 13:5-8

Scripture

Read John 13:1-11.

Reflection

It *is* good to give, but sometimes the act of receiving is a greater gift. It takes even more humility to put ourselves in the lower place, allowing ourselves to be cared for without complaint. . . . Unless we are willing to be one-down—to be the recipient of care—at least once in a while, we have no business demanding to be the person in power, always doing the caregiving.

—Jane Marie Thibault

Meditation

As I reached my nineties, I became all-the-more aware of diminished control. Loss of control had begun earlier, when I was no longer able to drive and had to rely on my wife or the community van to get to the store or to a doctor's appointment. That was a big blow to my ego, for I had always prided myself on being in control of my life. Now, I was experiencing the loss of freedom to move about and to choose what I did and when I did it.

I have learned how to receive care and rely upon others. I have neuropathy, use a walker, and am becoming increasingly feeble and frail. This means being helped out of my chair and getting help from strangers with taking a shower. At times, when I become frustrated in putting on leg braces, I have to call on my wife for help. I even have to have someone open doors for me and to get me on and off the van to do grocery shopping. At first, relying upon others felt embarrassing to me. I was distressed and even frightened. It seemed as though everything was spinning out of control. Now, I am beginning to accept reality and to understand that receiving is also a blessing.

Simon Peter learned that it was important to have his feet washed by Jesus and to receive Jesus' care. Peter had always seen himself as the man in control and the master of every circumstance. It was Peter who made the great confession that Jesus was the Messiah. But now, he had to learn to accept the care of his Lord in that dramatic moment in the upper room. Peter had to learn the blessing of receiving.

For most of my life, I had been the caregiver offering help and support, especially to people with dementia and their caregivers. Now, the shoe is on the other foot, and I am the one who needs care and support. I have learned to embrace my growing identity as a receiver. I have learned that receiving help graciously is a sacred practice. Instead of complaining about my loss of control, I am able to express gratitude to everyone who reaches out to help me. I could not exist without that care.

Prayer

Give me grace, dear God, to accept my need for care and to express gratitude to those who reach out to help me. Amen.

Mutual Caregiving

Bear one another's burdens, and in this way you will fulfill the law of Christ.

—Galatians 6:2

Scripture

Read Galatians 6:1-10.

Reflection

There are only four kinds of people in the world—those who have been caregivers, those who are currently caregivers, those who will be caregivers, and those who will need caregivers.

—Rosalynn Carter[8]

Meditation

In my long experience of caring for people with dementia and their caregivers, I became aware that caregiving and care-receiving can be a mutual spiritual path. As I cared for others with my presence and support, those with dementia often offered me deep spiritual truths as they spoke from their souls. This experience prepared me for mutual caregiving in my relationship with my wife. Marriage in later life calls for forging a new relationship for marriage partners. As mutual caregivers, we became interdependent, wherein neither partner is self-sufficient.

Caring for each other in our much later years becomes all-the-more crucial as old age brings its challenges. The actual tipping point can often be marked with some precision: a fall, an accident, cognitive decline, strokes, and other neurological issues mean that coping with the ordinary tasks of daily life is no longer possible without help. So, we need each other.

My wife, Alice Ann, who died recently, cared for many of my needs. She cleaned our apartment when we lived in independent living, worked in the kitchen, and assisted me as I tottered around on the brink of falling. Due to my anti-stroke medications, I had a few bleeds, and she was always there for me, to calm my fears and clean up my mess. She was totally supportive of my time spent in writing this book, and without that support, it never could have happened. Her death has left a large void in my life, as I struggle to live without her.

When we lived in independent living, I was the master grocery shopper, riding the van every week to supply us with food. At times, I was her handyman, and I tried to be a good listener, although at times I failed. I brought her books and reminded her of names she had forgotten. In her later years, she suffered from cognitive decline, so I reminded her of what I had said, answered the same questions from her many times, and even made notes for her. I tried to keep her informed of current events and family news as I worked on the computer. We shared the same religious and political views, which was so helpful, when the vast majority of the residents where we once lived held views that were different from ours.

For my wife and me, our relationship and mutual care-giving were grounded in unconditional love. We loved each other as we were, not for what others expected of us. I will always grieve the loss of such love in a marriage of mutual caregiving.

Prayer

Loving Parent, we bless you for late-life marriages. Amen.

Over-Helpfulness

All must test their own work; then that work,
rather than their neighbor's work, will become a
cause for pride. *For all must carry their own loads.*
—Galatians 6:4-5 (emphasis added)

Scripture

Read Galatians 6:1-10.

Reflection

This above all: to thine own self be true,
And it must follow, as the night the day,
Thou canst not then be false to any man.

—William Shakespeare[9]

No one saves us but ourselves.
No one can and no one may.
We ourselves must walk the path.

—Buddha[10]

Meditation

It seemed as if the apostle Paul contradicted himself in his counsel to the Galatian Christians. First, he told his readers to "bear one another's burdens" (6:2); and then, almost in the same breath, he told them to "carry their own loads" (v. 5). It is not a matter of *either/or* but *both/and*. In later life, we may be asked to care for our spouses or other people. At the same time, we need to care for ourselves. There are times when others may not be there to help us, so we need to learn to handle some things by ourselves, hard as that may be.

His name was Bob. He was a ninety-year-old friend who was confined to his wheelchair. Yet this did not prevent him from wheeling all over the community, always being present for chapel and meetings. I called him "Old King Cole," for he was indeed "a merry old soul." On one occasion, I reached out to push his wheelchair, and he quickly refused my help, saying, "I can do that myself!" Despite his handicap, he maintained some self-reliance. I found myself guilty of over-helpfulness. Bob died several years ago, but I still miss his cheerful spirit and determined self-reliance.

Despite the best of our intentions, it is easy to fall into the trap of being too intrusive when we try to help older people: We rush in to fix their problems, not being aware that they can handle them by themselves. Often, our need to assist older people who seem to be in distress is caused by our own need not to be anxious. To be around such people and their situations reminds us of our own vulnerability and the possibility that their handicaps may come true for us when we are older.

The best approach in offering help to older people is to determine whether the older person needs and wants our help or whether they can rely on their own strengths and abilities. We need to avoid giving unasked-for help or advice and trying to change people and instead trust the path God has chosen for them. We need to simply be with older people, accepting them with their frailties, and be available when they ask for our help.

Prayer

Caring God, help us to be gracious to those who reach out to help us; but also affirm our right to rely upon ourselves, and give us the wisdom to know the difference. Amen.

Adult Children and Aging Parents: Forging a New Relationship

As God's chosen ones, holy and beloved, clothe
yourself with compassion, kindness, humility,
meekness, and patience. Bear with one another.
—Colossians 3:12-13

Scripture

Read Matthew 15:1-9.

Reflection

For the task of a lifetime, how may I prepare?
None other has traveled this particular road,
With its history, its calling, and the weight of its load.
I'm both burdened and blessed for my parents to bear.

Will the day-to-day challenges bring forth my best?
Will my weaknesses taint this deep longing to care?
Can I cultivate courage to walk with them where
We must all make our passage through darkness, to rest?
                                    —Daniel C. Potts

Meditation

In a dispute with the Pharisees and scribes, Jesus chided them for disregarding the needs of their parents by declaring as "Corban"—"an offering to God"—the goods that ought to have been used to aid their parents (see Mark 7:1-13). Adult children need to care for their aging parents, but this care must be based on love, not contract.

The older claim is no longer valid that it is "payback" time, that adult children "owe" care for their aging parents as repayment, saying that their children owe them everything because their parents took care of them when they were children. These demands can lay heavy guilt trips upon the children.

The philosopher Jane English has said, "The relationship between children and their parents should be one of friendship characterized by mutuality rather than one of reciprocal favors." Expounding upon the work of Jane English, Harry R. Moody has written, "The vocabulary of 'friendship' offers the best description of what goes on in this relationship. . . . [Al]though there are many things that children should do for their parents, it is inappropriate and misleading to say that the children 'owe' their parents these things."[11]

The obligations of adult children toward their aging parents are those of friends, based upon the love between them and their parents. Children cannot and should not try to provide for all their parents' needs. Love's knowledge can provide a balance between the needs of the parents and the resources of their children. Forging this new relationship in later life protects adult children from needless guilt about caring for their parents as well as safeguards the parents' own needs and wishes.

Prayer

Loving Parent, as an older parent, may I not make excessive demands on my children but, with them, determine how and when love can meet our mutual needs. Amen.

STILL GRIEVING
THE LOSS OF A SPOUSE

Rachel died, and she was buried on the way to
Ephrath (that is, Bethlehem), and Jacob set up
a pillar at her grave; it is the pillar of Rachel's
tomb, which is there to this day.

—Genesis 35:19-20

Scripture

Read Genesis 29:9-12; 35:19-20.

Reflection

With you a part of me hath passed away;
For in the peopled forest of my mind
A tree made leafless by this wintry wind
Shall never don again its green array.
Chapel and fireside, country road and bay,
Have something of their friendliness resigned;

Another, if I would, I could not find,
And I am grown much older in a day.
                          —George Santayana[12]

Meditation

Once, I stood at a graveside in the dead of winter; the tent poles were clanging in the wind. Sad faces were fixed upon the casket. The couple had been married more than sixty years. Suddenly, the grieving widow cried out, "Don't leave me! I want to die too!" She seemed inconsolable.

Then, I was the pastor, offering comfort to this late-life widow. Now, I am the grieving husband. My wife of more than four decades died suddenly of a heart attack, and I know all too well how that grieving widow felt. For all those years, Alice Ann and I were devoted to each other as partners in this life. Now, she is gone, and I have lost my life companion. I feel pared down; part of me is missing. I feel like a lonely bird sitting on a barren twig, who has lost its voice.

Rachel was Jacob's dearest love, and he looked forward to spending the rest of his life with her. But instead, he found himself building a pillar at her grave and journeying on to Canaan without her, still numb with shock. Jacob's life had changed, and he would never be the same without Rachel. No doubt, he wished he could die and be buried with her.

Everyone grieves in his or her own way. Some prefer to bottle up their grief within themselves and share it with no one. Others, like me, need to vent their sorrow with family members or trusted friends. Grief never moves in a straight line. Just when we think the pain is over and life has regained some semblance of normalcy, grief rolls over us like a massive ocean wave. Old feelings of despair and loss resurface, and we become painfully aware of our loss, as mourning returns.

The apostle Paul offers wise counsel to the Corinthians who have experienced grief in their losses. As God has comforted them in their grief, they can offer that same comfort to others (see 2 Corinthians 1:3-4). I did not want to wallow in my grief and live as a recluse in my one-room apartment. So, with the help of the chaplain, I reached out to the other residents, living on three floors in Personal Care, where I now reside. Due to the COVID-19 virus, other than staff members, some of them rarely see anyone except a family member for an hour a week.

I have learned that most of the residents I visit are in their early- or late-nineties! Some are aware of my recent loss; some are not. But invariably, as we share our stories, these ninety-year-olds will talk about the loss of their spouse. They recall their lives together, and at times they even point out to me photos of their husband or wife, which linger on walls of their apartments. In my ministry of presence, these visits become sacred moments for me and them.

Dealing with the demands of grief preserves the memory of our loved one, but we discover we have become not only a healed victim but also a wounded healer.

Prayer

Comforter of those who mourn, I know that comfort. Now, help me reach out to others who mourn and offer my presence and comfort. Amen.

24

Being a Mentor

When they had crossed [the river], Elijah said to Elisha, "Tell me what I may do for you, before I am taken from you." Elisha said, "Please let me inherit a double share of your spirit." . . . [Elisha] picked up the mantle of Elijah that had fallen from him.

—2 Kings 2:9, 13

Scripture

Read 2 Kings 2:6-13.

Reflection

Show me a successful individual and I'll show you someone who had real positive influences in his or her life. I don't care what you do for a living—if you do it well I'm sure there was someone cheering you on or showing the way. A mentor.

—Denzel Washington[13]

In order to be a mentor, and an effective one, one must care. You must care.[14]

—Maya Angelou

Meditation

There are some excellent examples of mentoring in the Bible. The aged priest Eli, who was blind, was a mentor to the boy Samuel, who lived with him in the Temple. It was Eli who recognized that it was God calling Samuel in the night (see 1 Samuel 3). Elijah was the mentor of Elisha, who asked for "a double share of your spirit" as he took up the mantle of Elijah. The apostle Paul was a mentor to young Timothy, who accompanied Paul on his second and third missionary journeys.

In my college and seminary years, I was blessed by several professors who went the extra mile to be my mentors. Their concern for me went far beyond the classroom. Even though most of them have died, I still remember their kindness and constant support. They were there for me at some difficult times in my life. I believe my career, my teaching, and my writing never could have happened without them.

When I was a college professor, I had the opportunity to mentor many students. Some of them became teachers, following my example. I still hear from some of them, expressing their gratitude after all these years. However, at age ninety and confined to this place, my mentoring is now restricted to occasional emails or phone calls.

I have ten grandchildren, scattered across the country in five states. I rarely see most of them anymore, but I stay in touch with them too by phone and through emails. I like to believe that I still have some impact on their lives. Recently, I learned that my grandson Chris and his wife, Jessica, had my first great-grandson, Grayson, in May 2020. Grandson Patrick and his wife, Abby, also had a child, Noah, in June 2020, my second great-grandchild. My prayers surround these children following their births now, and they will continue as long as I am alive.

Prayer

God of all ages, I know that my mentoring of members of the coming generations is limited by my frailties and disabilities. May my heart recall precious moments when I was able to mentor others. Help me to remember those moments that brought so much meaning to my life. Amen.

Claiming the Mystery at Ninety

One cannot but be in awe when one contemplates the mysteries of eternity, of life, of the marvelous structure of reality. It is enough if one tries merely to comprehend a little of this mystery every day.

—Albert Einstein[1]

25

More Solitude

"But whenever you pray, go into your room and shut the door and pray to your Father who is in secret; and your Father who sees in secret will reward you."

—Matthew 6:6

Scripture

Read Matthew 6:5-13; Luke 10:38-42.

Reflection

Come now to the secret places of the soul.
Let us each inspect ourselves with care,
looking at the emotions which stir our
hearts and the thoughts which run through
our minds. Let us learn the essential goodness
of the heart from the heart itself.

—Morgan of Wales[2]

Meditation

As a boy of twelve, I recited from memory the Sermon on the Mount to a large congregation in the church where my father was the minister. Even now, I remember those timeless words of Jesus. Some of Jesus' words urged his disciples to find a secret place, to shut the door to all distractions and pray to the Father. At ninety, I find myself limiting social activity and spending more time in solitude.

During these moments, I begin my prayer by being silent. I lay aside all thoughts and open my whole being to God, the Ultimate Mystery, who by faith is within us. This is no easy task, as my "monkey mind" swings from one thought to another, as monkeys swing from tree to tree, rarely settling in one place. In the silence, I seek to be centered as the Divine Mystery touches my spirit and carries me beyond myself into pure awareness. That is my hope as I meditate.

Years ago, I heard a story about an overly talkative American tourist, who climbed a high mountain to seek wisdom from a guru who lived there. The tourist asked the guru, "Don't you get lonely up here all by yourself?" "No," replied the guru, "not until you came." At ninety, I need some social interaction; but more and more, I prefer my solitude.

In my earlier years of being older, I favored my "Martha" side, staying active with writing and volunteering for people with dementia and offering support for caregivers. I still needed that activity then to feel significant and needed. Now, I focus on my "Mary" side, where I can be still and listen to the Holy Presence. There is no need, any longer, to be productive but much more need to be contemplative.

Prayer

Jesus, as Mary sat in reverent silence to listen for your words, so may I go into my room, shut the door, and listen in silence for your eternal words. Amen.

26

Cosmic Awareness

When one turns to the Lord, the veil is removed. Now the Lord is the Spirit, and where the Spirit of the Lord is, there is freedom. And all of us, with unveiled faces, seeing the glory of the Lord as though reflected in a mirror, are being transformed into the same image from one degree of glory to another; for this comes from the Lord, the Spirit.

—2 Corinthians 3:16-18

Scripture

Read 2 Corinthians 3:12-18.

Reflection

It's not that we despair because we are going to die. We despair at
closing our eyes for the last time on the beauty of the world and

the people we love. And when we die, we slip into the
mystery;
we go to God in a way that has not entered human
imagination.
But ultimately and finally, there is the promise of
resurrection.
And then, anew, our eyes are opened.

—David M. Seymour

Meditation

At ninety, I have become all the more attentive to a cosmic
awareness where the veil between heaven and earth grows
thin, and where this world and the other world touch each
other. On Mount Sinai, Moses experienced the "thin place"
as the other world touched him (see Exodus 34). So dazzling
was the glory Moses experienced, he had to put a veil over
his face, so as not to blind the Israelites. And in the New
Testament, three disciples—Peter, James, and John—caught
a glimpse of heaven touching earth before their eyes. They
saw Jesus transformed with the glory of another world (see
Matthew 17:1-13).

Two epiphanies remain in my consciousness, when
heaven seemed to touch earth. I stood on the beach of the
island Iona, off the western coast of Scotland, in the year
2000. I was spellbound by the beauty of the moment: It
seemed as if heaven had come to earth. I could feel the presence of God in a real way, as I was mindful of Columba, the
Irish abbot and missionary, standing on that same beach,
reciting the Psalms.

A few years later, I walked around the ruins of the monastery of Tintern Abbey in Wales, founded in 1131 CE. If I really listened and watched, I could visualize monks rising for their morning prayers. Here, by the ruined walls of an ancient faith, I saw an eerie mist fill the skies above the abbey. At that moment, I remembered that for my Celtic ancestors, the mist was a symbol of God's presence, a threshold state in spirituality. I remembered the words of the English poet William Wordsworth, written in 1798 from a hill overlooking Tintern Abbey, that there is "a presence . . . / Whose dwelling is the light of setting suns, / And the round ocean, and the living air, / And the blue sky, and in the mind of man."[3] I felt transported to another world.

Now, only memories remain, but they are constant reminders that God does lift the veil between heaven and earth, and the unseen becomes seen.

Prayer

Thank you, Eternal God, for those incredible moments when the veil is lifted, and we are assured that there is a land beyond the stars. Amen.

Still a Mystery

I consider that the sufferings of this present time are not worth comparing with the glory about to be revealed to us. . . . For I am convinced that neither death, nor life . . . nor anything else in all creation, will be able to separate us from the love of God in Christ Jesus our Lord.
—Romans 8:18, 38-39

Scripture

Read Romans 8:18-39.

Reflection

And that is where the Problems of Evil begin. "If . . , why?," we ask. If God is truly immanent, and not just watching, why does our all-powerful, all-loving God not intervene more effectively in the troubling situations where humans are affected most? After all, God is agape love, and . . . love is supposed to act, not just observe.

—Thomas Ronald Vaughan[4]

Meditation

All my life, I have asked myself the eternal question, *Why do innocent people suffer?* If God does not cause suffering, God does still allow it. Why? At ninety years of life, I still ask that question, and the answer remains a mystery. Why did God allow a close friend and faithful pastor to die from cancer and leave a grieving family? Why did God let a baby girl die at childbirth and send her mother into endless despair? Why did God allow a brilliant woman to develop Alzheimer's disease and vanish into nothingness? How could a loving God let millions be infected with the COVID-19 virus in a pandemic has that killed, as of this writing, more than 1,000,000 people across the world?

In Albert Camus's novel *The Plague*, the Jesuit priest Father Paneloux at first preaches a powerful sermon and claims that the plague is God's punishment upon the people of Oran for their sinful ways. But when he witnesses the agonizing death of a child, he changes his mind. Now, he has no answer to the question of why the good suffer. All that remains for him is to accept God's plan or reject it, even though he cannot understand what that plan is.

None of the theories that attempt to resolve this issue of reconciling a God of love with innocent suffering solves the mystery. There was a time when I believed that unjust suffering was God's way of soul-making; but now I know that is a half-truth, as I realized all too well that often suffering can make a person bitter, not better.

The patriarch Job struggled with God's unfair treatment of his godly life but found no answer to his agonizing question of "Why?" But in a theophany at the end of the book of Job, he has a new and awesome experience of the "God beyond God": "I had heard of you by the hearing of the ear, but now my eye sees you" (42:5).

Ronald Vaughan, in his book *God and the Twelve Problems of Evil: Into Great Mystery*, concludes that God experiences the suffering, pain, and sorrow of God's children and participates in them in mysterious ways. That's about all the light I can see now around this dark question that still plagues me. But this I believe:

> In every pang that rends the heart
> The Man of Sorrows had a part.[5]

"For now we see in a mirror, dimly, but then we will see face to face. Now I know only in part; then I will know fully, even as I have been fully known" (1 Cor. 13:12).

Prayer

Dear God, when I wonder about why good people suffer, all I can see now is puzzling reflections in a mirror. So, I claim the mystery and believe that you suffer when we suffer and that one day I will see clearly. Amen.

STILL VITAL AND GREEN

Even in old age they will still produce fruit;
they will remain vital and green.
—Psalm 92:14, NLT

Scripture

Read Proverbs 31:10-31.

Reflection

Oh, my God, my heavenly King,
All day will I Your praises sing.
In the morning, in the night,
Keep me in Your holy light.
When darkness overshadows me,
I know You, always, there will be,
Casting rays of light so bright
To sustain me in your holy light.

. . . .

Fear on me no longer has its hold;
The cares of this world grow ever cold.
Always, upward in Your sight,
I will rise to Your holy light.
                    —Dorothy Ivan Manzlak (1920–2020)

Meditation

The psalmist believed that some people in old age remained vital and green. That is surely true of two particular older women, friends of mine in this community. Dorothy was one hundred years old when she died. To the end of her life, although extremely frail, she was mentally sharp, and she wrote religious poetry. Margaret is ninety years old, still drives her own car, and has accumulated a wealth of wisdom from her experience and world travels. Both of them share their wisdom and spiritual insight with others in the community. Dorothy used to share her poetry, usually quoting it from memory to residents and her care aides. Margaret always enlightens discussions with her encyclopedic knowledge and insights.

Jean Vanier has called such people "community's hidden treasures." He describes them in the following way:

> They have the wonder of a child, but the wisdom of maturity as well. . . . Their freedom of heart and their acceptance of their limitations and weaknesses make them people whose radiance illuminated the whole community.[6]

Such are Dorothy and Margaret, who exemplify the characteristics of the worthy woman in Proverbs 31: "Strength and dignity are her clothing, and she laughs at the time to come" (v. 25). They remind me of Eleanor Roosevelt's words, "Beautiful young people are accidents of nature, but beautiful old people are works of art."[7]

I have often said that the three temptations of older people are to decline, to whine, and to recline. But there is a fourth option, a worthwhile one: to shine with the Spirit. Dorothy and Margaret have transcended old age as a time of bitterness and complaints, and they have shined with the Spirit.

Prayer

Ancient of Days, thank you for blessing this community with ninety-year-old people who bear witness to grace and beauty at such an old age. Amen.

29

LEAVING A SHADOW

Yet more than ever believers were added to the Lord, great numbers of both men and women, so that they even carried out the sick into the streets, and laid them on cots and mats, in order that Peter's shadow might fall on some of them as he came by.

—Acts 5:14-15

Scripture

Read John 14:25-31.

Reflection

The Body of
B. Franklin, Printer;
Like the Cover of an old Book,
Its Contents torn out,
And Stript of its Lettering & Gilding,

Lies here, Food for Worms.
But the Work shall not be lost,
For it will as he believ'd
appear once more
In a new and more elegant Edition
Corrected and improved
By the Author.

—Benjamin Franklin,
self-penned epitaph[8]

Meditation

Our lives cast shadows as long as we live. These are the marks we leave on this earth by our passing. These are the memories of us in the minds and hearts of those we have loved and who have loved us. These shadows touch loved ones long after we are gone. They are the legacy we leave for future generations.

Luke records that in the early church, they carried the sick on mats and cots, so that Peter's shadow might fall upon them. Peter's shadow was for healing (see Acts 5:12-15). We all die and don't live forever. But our goal should be to leave shadows that will.

The American statesman Benjamin Franklin wrote,

If you wou'd not be forgotten
As soon as you are dead and rotten,
Either write things worth reading,
or do things worth the writing.[9]

Franklin did both, leaving a shadow that still falls upon our republic. I like to believe that the books I wrote on the spirituality of aging are worth reading and will live on after I am gone, albeit eventually landing on library shelves.

The Greek philosopher Pericles (495 BCE–429 BCE) wrote, "What you leave behind is not what is engraved in stone monuments, but what is woven into the lives of others."[10] I believe the shadow I will leave for future generations is how I have helped others. I want to believe that like Peter, my shadow will be one of healing the hurt and pain of many people whose lives I touched.

As I meditate on my long life, many memories return of ways I reached out to help others. My shadow falls upon the poorest, the sickest, and the oldest of our society, whom I have tried to help and be present to their needs. For the past forty years, I have devoted myself to caring for people with dementia and their overburdened caregivers. That is a legacy that will outlive me.

Prayer

I bless you, O caring God, for people whose shadows of healing fell on me and for the opportunity to let my shadow fall on people in need. Amen.

30

Attachment to Earlier Generations

Look to the rock from which you were hewn,
   and to the quarry from which you were dug.
Look to Abraham your father
   and to Sarah who bore you.
                              —Isaiah 51:1-2

Scripture

Read Psalm 51:1-3.

Reflection

In remembering life in our family of origin and the stories that often are kept hidden in closets and closed minds, we discover the forces that made us what we are today, helping to put our lives in perspective . . . Your individual story is set within a framework of family history of rules, customs, traditions, taboos, and ways of interacting that shape personalities.

—Richard L. Morgan[11]

Meditation

In much-later old age, a greater attachment develops to earlier generations. What becomes important is not so much your individual self but yourself as an ongoing part of the stream of life. Ancestors become closer and more valued. The Vietnamese Buddhist monk Thích Nhất Hanh wrote, "If you look deeply into the palm of your hand, you will see your parents and all generations of your ancestors. All of them are alive in this moment. Each is present in your body. You are the continuation of each of these people."[12] And some Native American cultures say that the spirits of ancestors appear to dying people as guides into the next world.

I have researched the family heritage of both my mother and father, the Lyons and the Morgans, and I have even traveled to Wales and Scotland in search of my roots. As I read the stories of my ancestors, I marvel at what they had to overcome: the death of a child, rejection for the ministry, serious illness, divorce, strokes, crossing the ocean to immigrate to another world. It is strange to me that I too have suffered some of these same crises. I believe my ancestors, though not present, guide my thoughts and actions.

Now, as I have reached the age of ninety and beyond, these ancestors are more than pictures on my wall or names in family histories. If I pause and am quiet, I can almost hear Grandfather Morgan preaching the gospel at Westminster Chapel and Papa Lyon calling sinners to "hit the sawdust trail" and repent of their sins. I hear my father's melodious British voice from the pulpit, an echo of his father. I am present at that moment when my mother and Grandmother Lyon rejoice at their reunion with Aunt Ruth. My aunt walked miles through the snow to that reunion after being freed from twenty-five years in a mental hospital.

I liken my life to a quilt. I started with scraps of material passed on to me by my genes and family history. I have added my own materials to this quilt. All these pieces have become the pattern of my life.

Prayer

Dear God, I thank you for my ancestors, who become more real to me in my later years. May I so live as to honor their memories and provide inspiration for future generations. Amen.

DECREASED FEAR OF DEATH

If we live, we live to the Lord, and if we die, we die to the Lord; so then, whether we live or whether we die, we are the Lord's.

—Romans 14:8

Scripture

Read Romans 14:7-9.

Reflection

For to fear death, gentlemen, is nothing else than to think one is wise when one is not; for it is thinking that one knows what one does not know. For no one knows whether death be not even the greatest of all blessings to man.

—Plato[13]

Even the bravest soul has felt the absence of God. The loss can last days or years.

Yet, there are moments when the veil is lifted, and you understand you are not alone but surrounded by the presence of the Holy. In Celtic language, there are "thin places" where if only for a moment, the veil between time and eternity is lifted and one can feel presence of another dimension breaking into this one. At this moment, one feels and understands the presence of the Holy. Such times last a lifetime and can bring solace and light into the darkest corners.

—John C. Morgan

Meditation

Since I was a boy of six, the fear of death has hounded my days and my nights. My first brush with death occurred when I suffered lobar pneumonia as a young boy and overheard Dr. Scott tell my parents, "No point in taking Dick to the hospital. When the crisis comes, he will either live or die." I was terrified. Later in my life, I survived an automobile accident and complications from surgery that brought me to the edge. Death has never been a stranger. It has been a presence that walks the road of life with me, and it shadows my every thought and feeling.

At my much-older, current age, the fear of death has lessened for me. I am still afraid of dying, and I pray that I will be spared the pain and agony of dying in a hospital or a nursing home. But I no longer fear death. Now, death is a journey into a new life of peace and joy. Socrates remarked as he neared death that if there is nothing beyond death, he wouldn't know; and if there *is* something, he would not be afraid.

As for dying, I wonder whether I will die suddenly in the night, as did my father; or, like my mother, will I die a slow, painful death, a patient of hospice? In whatever manner death comes, I hope to be ready and to die with dignity and peace.

As to the life beyond death, I still cling to the words of British historian Herbert Butterfield: "Hold to Christ, and for the rest be totally uncommitted."[14] I have long believed that as Jesus was in the forty days between Easter and the Ascension—present with the disciples and transformed—so we shall be in the next life; resurrected; a glorified existence. "What we do know is this: when he is revealed, we will be like him, for we will see him as he is" (1 John 3:2).

So, freed by Christ's love, which casts out fear of death, I try to live each day to the fullest, believing, "If we live, we live to the Lord, and if we die, we die to the Lord; so then, whether we live or whether we die, we are the Lord's" (Rom. 14:8).

Prayer

Lord, help me to face death with courage, praying, "Father, into thy hands I commit my spirit." Amen.

32

LOVE:
THE ULTIMATE REALITY

Now faith, hope, and love abide, these three;
and the greatest of these is love.

—1 Corinthians 13:13

Scripture

Read 1 Corinthians 13.

Reflection

For People Ageing

God of the unknown,
as age draws in on us, irresistible as the tide,
make our life's last quarter the best that there has been.
As our strength ebbs, release our inner vitality,
all you have taught us over the years;
as our energy diminishes

increase our compassion, and educate our prayer.
You have made us human to share your divine life;
grant us the first-fruits;
make our life's last quarter the best that there has been.
—*A New Zealand Prayer Book*[15]

Meditation

Thirty years ago, when I wrote *No Wrinkles on the Soul*, one of the last meditations I wrote was "Love Is the Last Word." Since that time when I was much younger, I have experienced many of the issues of being much older. But I still believe that love is the final reality when all else crumbles to dust. The apostle Paul wrote, "Therefore we do not lose heart. Though outwardly we are wasting away, yet inwardly we are being renewed day by day" (2 Cor. 4:16, NIV). The years have taken their toll on my body, but my spirit remains new and vital.

Henry Drummond, author of *The Greatest Thing in the World*, has said, "As I look back I see standing out above all the life that has gone, four or five short experiences when the love of God reflected itself in . . . some small act of love of mine, and these seem to be the things which alone of all one's life abide."[16] How true! Everything else in my life is transitory and soon will become memories in my life's memoir.

The love that others have given me and the love I have given to others will remain. Those lifesaving moments when someone was there for me with unconditional love will remain. Those few, short experiences when I was there for someone with unconditional love will remain.

The greatest of these is *love*. It never fails. It is the ultimate word.

Prayer

Thank you, loving God, that as the evening of life comes, only love remains. Amen.

EPILOGUE

Living Up to Death

"When you were young, you were able to do as
you liked. . . . But when you are old, you will
stretch out your hands . . . and others . . . will
take you where you don't want to go."
— John 21:18, NLT

I n my earlier book *With Faces to the Evening Sun: Faith
Stories from the Nursing Home,* I told the story of a woman
who was moved from a comfortable apartment with caregivers ready to heed her every need to one room in assisted living. When she entered her new "home," she looked around
and moaned, "Has my life come to this?"

Since I have written this book, my life has drastically
changed. At first, I could also ask, "Has my life come to
this?" In the midst of the COVID-19 virus pandemic, I was
uprooted from my home in Independent Living, where I had
lived for seventeen years. I had two days to pack up whatever
I could take and be placed in an apartment called Supportive Living. The move was necessitated by my wife's need for
additional care after back surgery and by my own increased
frailty and risk of falling at age ninety-one. What made the

move easier was that our daughter was able to arrange for my wife and me to be together in the same apartment.

This new place reminded me of a nursing home. I had served as a chaplain in two nursing homes in North Carolina, and I quickly recognized the similarities. Then, I was an outsider; now, I had become an insider, subject to all the changes and demands of Supportive Living. Once, I had visited people with Alzheimer's, dementia, and Parkinson's; now, I was living with them in a halfway house between Personal Care and Skilled Nursing.

My situation was compounded by the COVID-19 virus. A staff member had tested positive for the virus; this meant that my wife and I were quarantined in our apartment for sixteen days, which exacerbated our sense of feeling confined. I confess that at first, I faced each day with a sense of terrible dread. I had lost my identity and seemed to have no purpose in living, so I endlessly paced the floors of my apartment as if I were in jail. Every day, I read Dietrich Bonhoeffer's *Letters and Papers from Prison*. I suffered from what Frits de Lange calls "a silent negativity."

It is now three months later, and some of the fog has lifted. But the major changes in life have remained. We live in a society where people are living much longer, and it may well be that some of you will face what happened to me so abruptly. As it was with me, the tipping point was debilities of old age, which may well occur to you.

Some older people remain in denial that what happened to me could ever happen to them. If you are blessed, you may go into the good night on cruise control. But I believe many of you will face a similar upheaval at some point in your life.

In defining and reflecting upon these changes, perhaps you will realize what you or an aging parent will be facing and be ready to meet them.

From Independence to Dependence

It did not take long for me to realize that my freedom had been replaced by the control of others. The day I entered Supportive Living, my medications were taken from me, and they were controlled and dispensed by the nurse four times a day. Even my medical appointments had to be made by a clerk and then only with the prior approval of the facilities director. No longer could I plan my life and take long walks about the lovely grounds of Independent Living. Now, I could only walk down the hall to the community dining room or take a few measured steps on an outside path. I soon learned that I had little autonomy and that I was at the mercy of nurses and nursing assistants. Even our finances were now controlled by our adult children, after many long years when I managed them myself.

From Privacy to Interruptions

Every day, people pop in and out of our apartment at all hours of the day and sometimes at night. Some enter without knocking. This has been hard for an introvert like me who values his privacy and always guarded it fiercely. For the first time in my long life, I went to the community shower room, sat in a big chair, and stripped naked as a young certified nursing assistant turned on the shower faucet. All modesty flew out the window. Often, you are awakened early in the morning by a nursing assistant to take your vital signs.

From Community Life to a New Parish

While my wife and I lived in Independent Living, we always had our cadre of friends for lively conversation. We were a true community. But no longer. I soon learned that there is little community life here—only much-older people living out their last days. Only a few of the residents would engage in conversation, so I reached out to the aides and related to them. A mark of a spiritual person is to turn strangers into friends. These hardworking, underpaid people would often stop and linger for a while in our apartment. This developed into a ministry of caring. It became a mutual blessing. For them, it proved a time of sanctuary; for me, I was assured that I could still be vital and that I still had a purpose in a new and different parish. I soon bonded with the nursing assistants, and I have listened to their stories. I've already given many copies of my books to them. Some are in training to be nurses or physician assistants.

From Caregiving to Care Receiving

Although I alluded to this earlier, my move to Supportive Living has accentuated this change. Formerly, I was the caregiver: I counseled students, tried to care for my wife, and offered pastoral care for people with dementia. Now, I find myself in a different role, allowing myself to be cared for without complaint. I have learned to accept care in being lifted from my chair, given a shower, and having a caregiver make my bed and do my laundry, tasks that I used to do for myself. No words can express my deep gratitude to these nurses and nursing assistants whose loving care have made life more bearable.

This is a fourth state of life, which can entail loss of choice, autonomy, self-expression, and pleasure, all of which I face every day, But I am determined not to succumb to these threats and to try to live with joy and purpose. I am living up to the point of death, and I am striving to say, with the apostle Paul, "I have learned the secret of living in every situation" (Phil. 4:12, NLT).

Postscript: In the early fall of 2020, my beloved wife, Alice Ann, died of heart failure. We had moved to Supportive Living so that she might receive additional help with her heart issues. I had a lesser role as her caregiver and had to be content with helping her in small ways, any way I could. No words of mine could ever express my gratitude for the loving care she received from nurses and aides; these angels of mercy, although underpaid and at times understaffed, taught me what unconditional love really is, as they cared for her with love and even a sense humor.

I cannot help but grieve the loss of a lover, confidante, and life partner. Alice Ann and I had lived in a world of mutual love, interdependence, and shared life for over four decades. I remain heartbroken at her loss, which changes my life as I grieve the loss of my caregiving role. I have no idea of what lies beyond in the few years left to me. In time, I may make my way to offer my caregiving to others where I live, in a new place. If so, I have had a blessed example of unconditional love here at Redstone. I will long remember the constant and unselfish care these caregivers gave my wife in her last days on this earth.

AFTERWORD

Lynda Everman and Donald J. Wendorf

It was early June 2020. We hadn't heard from our friend Richard Morgan for several days, and we were beginning to get concerned when we saw his name come up on the phone caller ID.

With Richard's opening words, "Life can change in a twinkling of an eye!" our sense of relief quickly turned to apprehension and then sadness. Our friend was in trouble.

Richard shared that in the span of one short week, his wife, Alice Ann, had been hospitalized for severe back pain and that he was now in the midst of packing up the belongings in their apartment of seventeen years in a senior-care facility for a move to a different facility, one that would provide them with greater care. Alice Ann was hospitalized on a Monday; they would be moving on Friday. All of this, while being shut down during the COVID-19 pandemic, at the age of ninety-one and while having to use a walker due to his increasing bouts with neuropathy that made him a serious fall risk.

On the face of it, this move, while abrupt, seemed sensible and even welcome, as the new community had the capacity to offer higher levels of care, relieving Richard and Alice Ann of tasks that had become increasingly difficult as more and more, they faced a series of health challenges. They began the lonely, stressful, and exhausting process of learning new people, new procedures, new locations, new ways to live as fully as possible . . . again. Always another "again," despite already being so tired. But one of Richard's mantras is "Always we begin again."

Over the next few weeks, we stayed in touch by phone with our friends as they courageously faced numerous setbacks and began to settle in, grateful for increased help but also dealing with unexpected changes and grieving major losses. From afar, we witnessed their faith, their love for each other, and their resiliency. During the coronavirus quarantine, we jokingly referred, along with them, to their new apartment in Personal Care as their "cell," and we watched them carve a path forward that would include new, meaningful connections and continued purpose. There followed a series of highly restrictive quarantines, as others there tested positive for the virus.

But how does one possess the strength of character and resiliency to face such difficult times? These are the lessons Richard shares in this book, as he writes about those traits and spiritual practices we develop and cultivate over a lifetime in order to sustain us into old age and into the "oldest old" age: humility; gratitude; vulnerability; meaningful intent and purpose; integrity; compassion; patience; comfort with solitude; the ability to find positives and good in the most-trying circumstances; the capacity to deal with increasing losses of friends, abilities, possessions, and autonomy. While not easily acquired, these traits are the building blocks of resiliency. They are the foundation for developing even more old-age survival attributes such as learning to receive as well as to give, understanding and valuing these interactions as the same thing. Gracious receiving bestows a blessing, while giving nurtures the giver as well.

On October 6, 2020, Richard called with the news that his beloved wife, Alice Ann, had died unexpectedly of congestive heart failure the day after a bad fall. He was in shock and felt devastated, overwhelmed, and painfully sad. Once more, he faced another "again" with another abrupt move to another new apartment upstairs, with the loss of his new friends downstairs and a new life without his wife of forty-two years. Another "again," once again.

So, while this is, indeed, an unchartered time for our friend, we know that because he has done the work, he will continue to thrive. Richard still looks to find new goals and meaning, new ways to create and accomplish. The mark of a spiritual person, according to Richard, is to turn strangers into friends, which he does with the residents and the staff in his new home. And the mark of a resilient person is to go forward in spite of adversity. He continues to see opportunities for developing new ministries, new things to write about, and new ways to serve others. Within three days of losing Alice Ann, he told us, "I project my life into the future as a widower in a new place."

We often think of Richard as we hike in the woods around Birmingham, Alabama, especially when we see very old trees that have weathered innumerable storms, droughts, and winds. These trees may have broken and split branches; they may share their life force with all sorts of vines and lichen and fungi and critters, and even be bent over almost to the ground. But they are—as Richard is, and as we all can be—"still vital and green" and full of new growth, and they will continue to be beautiful a little longer.

> They will be like trees
> that stay healthy and fruitful,
>   even when they are old.
>
> —Psalm 92:14, CEV

SCRIPTURE INDEX

Old Testament

New Testament

NOTES

FOREWORD—Harry R. (Rick) Moody

1. Plato, *The Republic*, translated by Benjamin Jowett, accessed at http://classics.mit.edu/Plato/republic.2.i.html.
2. "Compression of Morbidity" theory introduced in 1980 by Dr. James Fries, professor of medicine at Stanford University: https://palliative.stanford.edu/overview-of-palliative-care/compression-of-morbidity-theory.

PREFACE

1. *Meditations with Meister Eckhart,* introduction and versions by Matthew Fox (Rochester, VT: Bear & Company, 1983), 53.

BEING NINETY

1. Edward Kendall, "Jean Vanier's 10 Rules for Life to Become More Human," *The Tablet* (September 14, 2018), https://www.thetablet.co.uk/news/9747/jean-vanier-s-10-rules-for-life-to-become-more-human-.
2. Frits de Lange, *Loving Later Life: An Ethics of Aging* (Grand Rapids, MI: Eerdmans Publishing, 2015), 107.
3. Jane Marie Thibault and Richard L. Morgan, *Pilgrimage into the Last Third of Life: 7 Gateways to Spiritual Growth* (Nashville, TN: Upper Room Books, 2012), 19.

4. Will Willimon, *Aging: Growing Old in Church* (Grand Rapids, MI: Baker Academic, 2020), 4.

5. Alfred, Lord Tennyson, "Ulysses," *Norton Anthology of English Literature*, 10th ed., vol. 2 (New York, NY: W. W. Norton & Company, Inc., 2018), 736.

6. Joan Erikson, as quoted by Stephen S. Hall, *Wisdom: From Philosophy to Neuroscience* (New York: Vintage Books, 2011), 240.

7. Judith Gusky, "Why Aren't They Screaming? A Counselor's Reflection on Aging," *Counseling Today*, April 1, 2012, https://ct.counseling.org/2012/04/why-arent-they-screaming-a-counselors-reflection-on-aging/.

8. Daniel Goleman, "Erikson, in His Own Old Age, Expands His View of Life," *The New York Times*, June 14, 1988, https://movies2.nytimes.com/books/99/08/22/specials/erikson-old.html.

9. Seneca the Younger, AZ Quotes, https://www.azquotes.com/author/19765-Seneca_the_Younger/tag/aging.

10. Robert Browning, "Rabbi Ben Ezra" (1897), stanza I, lines 1–4.

11. Penelope Lively, *Dancing Fish and Ammonites: A Memoir* (London: Penguin Books, 2015), 1, 8.

12. John Leland, *Happiness Is a Choice You Make: Lessons from a Year Among the Oldest Old* (New York: Sarah Crichton Books, 2018), 4.

13. Leland, *Happiness Is a Choice You Make*, 202.

BECOMING ONESELF AT NINETY

1. Malcolm Cowley, *The View from 80* (New York: The Viking Press, 1980), 73–74.

2. Richard L. Morgan, *No Wrinkles on the Soul: A Book of Readings for Older Adults* (Nashville, TN: Upper Room Books, 2002), 46.

3. Marcus Tullius Cicero, *Cato Maior de Senectute*, translated from Latin, accessed at http://penelope.uchicago.edu/Thayer/E/Roman/Texts/Cicero/Cato_Maior_de_Senectute/text*.html.

4. Margareta Magnusson, *The Gentle Art of Swedish Death Cleaning: How to Free Yourself and Your Family from a Lifetime of Clutter* (New York, NY: Scribner, 2018), 1, 101.

5. Kathleen Fischer, *Winter Grace: Spirituality and Aging*, (Nashville, TN: Upper Room Books, 1998), 8.

6. Rick Moody, cited by Frits de Lange, *Loving Later Life: An Ethics of Aging* (Grand Rapids, MI: Eerdmans Publishing, 2015), 9.

7. Susan Jacoby, *Never Say Die: The Myth and Marketing of the New Old Age* (New York: Vintage, 2012), 190–92.

8. Fischer, *Winter Grace*, 8.

9. Frits de Lange, *Loving Later Life: An Ethics of Aging* (Grand Rapids, MI: Eerdmans Publishing, 2015), 8.

10. Breton Fisherman's Prayer Plaque, John F. Kennedy Presidential Library and Museum, https://www.jfklibrary.org/asset-viewer/breton-fishermans-prayer-plaque.

RELATING TO OTHERS AT NINETY

1. Common English translation of Albert Schweitzer, essay entitled "Influence," in *Aus meiner Kindheit und Jugendzeit* (Munich, Germany: C. H. Beck, 1924).

2. W. B. Yeats, "The Municipal Gallery Revisited," *The Collected Poems of W. B. Yeats* (Ware, Hertfordshire, U. K.: Wordsworth Editions Limited, 1994), 276–77. Text by W. B. Yeats © copyright by Michael B. Yeats.

3. William Shakespeare, *Richard II*, act 2, scene 3, line 46.

4. Brenda Griffin Warren, "Celts to the Creche: St. Brigid of Kildare," https://saintsbridge.org/2013/12/11/celts-to-the-creche-st-brigid-of-kildare.

5. Thomas Merton, *Conjectures of a Guilty Bystander*, Image Classics edition (New York: Penguin Random House, 1968), 81.

6. Ben Witherington, "The Senility Prayer," http://ben witherington.blogspot.com/2007/09/when-you-havent-got-prayer.html.

7. Blaise Pascal, common paraphrase of English translation of *Pensées*, section 2, "The Misery of Man Without God," 139.

8. Rosalynn Carter, written testimony before the Senate Special Committee on Aging, https://www.cartercenter.org/news/editorials_speeches/rosalynn-carter-committee-on-aging-testimony.html.

9. William Shakespeare, *Hamlet*, act 1, scene 3.

10. Buddha, modern characterization of teachings around quote, "We Ourselves Must Walk the Path," https://www.daniellem-lasusa.com/blog-private/we-ourselves-must-walk-the-path.

11. Harry R. Moody, *Ethics in an Aging Society* (Baltimore, MD: Johns Hopkins University Press, 1992), 121.

12. George Santayana, "To W. P." c. 1883–1893; https://www.gutenberg.org/files/49721/49721-h/49721-h.htm.

13. Denzel Washington, "The Mentors He'll Never Forget," *Guideposts*, posted on Jan. 1, 2007, https://www.guideposts.org/better-living/positive-living/the-mentors-hell-never-forget.

14. Maya Angelou, from public service announcement in support of National Mentoring Month; https://sites.sph.harvard.edu/wmy/celebrities/maya-angelou.

CLAIMING THE MYSTERY AT NINETY

1. Albert Einstein, cited in "Quotes on the Wonder of Being," http://quotesonthewonderofbeing.blogspot.com/2008/08/quotes-on-wonder-of-existence-and-why.html.
2. Robert Van de Weyer, *The Letters of Pelagius*, quoted in Frank MacEowen, *The Mist-Filled Path: Celtic Wisdom for Exiles, Wanderers, and Seekers* (San Francisco: New World Library, 2002), 205.
3. William Wordsworth, "Lines Written a Few Miles Above Tintern Abbey" (1798), http://www.gutenberg.org/files/9622/9622-h/9622-h.htm#poem23.
4. Thomas Ronald Vaughan, *God and the Twelve Problems of Evil: Into Great Mystery* (Eugene, OR: Resources Publications, Wipf and Stock, 2020), 19.
5. Michael Bruce, "Where High the Heavenly Temple Stands" (ca. 1764).
6. Jean Vanier, *Community and Growth* (New York: Paulist Press, 1989), 140–41.
7. Eleanor Roosevelt, quoted in "Wit & Wisdom," *The Week* 13 (641) (November 1, 2013), 15.
8. Benjamin Franklin, self-penned epitaph, "Benjamin Franklin: In His Own Words," Library of Congress, https://www.loc.gov/exhibits/franklin/bf-trans61.html.
9. Benjamin Franklin, *Poor Richard's Almanack*, 1738, cited in "Either Write Things Worth Reading or Do Things Worth the Writing," Quote Investigator, https://quoteinvestigator.com/2016/04/27/worth/.
10. "Pericles," Wikiquote, https://en.wikiquote.org/wiki/Pericles.
11. Richard L. Morgan, *Remembering Your Story: Creating Your Own Spiritual Autobiography*, Revised Edition (Nashville, TN: Upper Room Books, 2002), 66.

12. Thích Nhất Hanh, quoted in Frederick Buechner, *Telling Secrets: A Memoir* (San Francisco: HarperOne, 1992), 30.

13. Plato, *Apology of Socrates*; http://www.perseus.tufts.edu /hopper/text?doc=Perseus%3Atext%3A1999.01.0170%3Ate xt%3DApol.%3Apage%3D29.

14. Herbert Butterfield, *Christianity and History*, quoted by C. T. McIntire, "Modern Pioneers: Herbert Butterfield," Christian History Institute, https://christianhistoryinstitute.org/ magazine/article/modern-pioneers-herbert-butterfield.

15. "For People Ageing," *A New Zealand Prayer Book—He Karakia Mihinare o Aotearnoa*, The Anglican Church in Aotearnoa, New Zealand and Polynesia. Used with permission.

16. Henry Drummond, *The Greatest Thing in the World: Experience the Enduring Power of Love* (Ada, MI: Revell, Baker Publishing, 2011), 52–53.

SUGGESTED READING

Chittister, Joan. *The Gift of Years: Growing Older Gracefully.* New York: BlueBridge, 2008.

de Lange, Frits. *Loving Later Life: An Ethics of Aging.* Grand Rapids, MI: Wm. B. Eerdmans, 2015.

Erikson, Erik H. *The Life Cycle Completed.* New York: W. W. Norton & Co., 1995.

Fischer, Kathleen. *Winter Grace: Spirituality for the Later Years.* New York: Paulist Press, 1985; reprinted by Upper Room Books.

Griffin, Emilie. *Green Leaves for Later Years: The Spiritual Path of Wisdom.* Downers Grove, IL: IVP Books, 2012.

Jacoby, Susan. *Never Say Die: The Myth and Marketing of the New Old Age.* New York: Vintage Books, 2012.

Leland, John. *Happiness Is a Choice You Make: Lessons from a Year Among the Oldest Old.* New York: Sarah Chricton Books, 2018.

Lem, Ellyn A. *Gray Matters: Finding Meaning in the Stories of Later Life.* New Brunswick, NJ: Rutgers University Press, 2020.

Palmer, Parker J. *On the Brink of Everything: Grace, Gravity, and Getting Old.* San Francisco: Berrett-Koehler Publishers, 2018.

Robinson, John. C. *The Three Secrets of Aging: A Radical Guide (Psssst—It Ain't Over Yet).* Winchester, UK: John Hunt Publishing Ltd., 2012.

Scott, Susan Carol. *Still Praying After All These Years: Meditations for Later Life.* Nashville, TN: Upper Room Books, 2019.

Thibault, Jane Marie and Richard L. Morgan. *Pilgrimage into the Last Third of Life: 7 Gateways to Spiritual Growth.* Nashville, TN: Upper Room Books, 2012.

Tornstam, Lars. *Gerotranscendence: A Developmental Theory of Positive Aging.* New York: Springer Publishing Company, 2005.

Weber, Robert L. and Carol Orsborn. *The Spirituality of Age: A Seeker's Guide to Growing Older.* Rochester, VT: Park Street Press, 2015.

Willimon, Will. *Aging: Growing Old in Church.* Grand Rapids, MI: Baker Academic, 2020.